To Lynn—
Love,
Connie

FALLING UP

Connie Carey has taken the unimaginable tragedy of her father's suicide and fashioned a rare gift for anyone whose life is marred by similar devastation. Through her transparent confessions of her own emotional journey, she gently leads and nudges the reader toward hope and healing. Her practical and concise steps of action declare the authenticity of her experience and reveal the triumph of emerging on the other side, borne in the arms of the Heavenly Father. This is an exceptional book, well-written, insightful, and thought-provoking.

MARY PERDUE
Former First Lady of the State of Georgia

Falling Up is an incredible story of faith and triumph that inspires readers to lay down their doubts and fears and trust in God who longs to heal their hurts. You will learn much from Connie Carey. I'm privileged to call her a friend.

MICCA CAMPBELL
Proverbs 31 Ministries Conference Speaker
Author of *An Untroubled Heart*

Connie's creative ability to weave a personal fun story into her journey with crippling grief and God's Word keeps you engaged, encouraged and equipped to "fall up." Her tools, F.A.L.L., will help anyone experiencing loss or disappointment, and I personally found them helpful for my own pain. *Falling Up* will be a resource I will share over and over again!

JUDY PATTERSON
Executive Editor, WomensMinistry.net,
A Service of Jennifer Rothschild Ministries

If you have experienced loss, and you have, if you are breathing, Connie's book is for you. She writes from her own personal experience of the devastating loss that resulted from her father's suicide. Her writing style is such that you are drawn into the Biblical principles she embraces. Having been a pastoral counselor for some 30 years, as well as a pastor for even more years, I can tell you that reading Connie's book will be like a balm to your sore and weary soul. She will help you understand that there is life beyond your deepest loss and grief.

REV. MAC GODDARD
Pastor, Counselor, Author and Lecturer

Falling Up is a rare treat of biblically sound wisdom, engaging stories, and joy-filled humor. I found myself saying, "Amen," laughing, and crying all in the same paragraph! Connie does an excellent job sharing her own journey while offering hope to those who desire to trust Christ and gaze heavenward when life seems to fall apart. I heartily recommend to friends and clients the powerful truth that is packaged so well in this delightful read.

SHERRI HALL
Director/Counselor, Creative Counseling Solutions for Women

If you are looking for a helpful and practical resource on navigating the emotional, mental and spiritual challenges brought on by the arrival of grief, you have found it here in Connie Carey's book, *Falling Up*. With transparency, levity, candor and, perhaps most importantly, faithfulness to Scripture, she has put together an excellent companion to help us walk through the inevitable season of heartbreak we all must face.

DAN DARDEN
Director/Counselor, Christian Counseling Services

DEDICATION

This book is dedicated to you, my friend.

While I don't know your name, God does.

*I believe He led you to pick up this book
because He wants to give you a new
perspective of what He is graciously, lovingly
doing behind the scenes of your suffering.*

*My prayer is that you will trust Him with
the pieces of your puzzle that don't
make sense at the moment.*

*May God grant you the grace to FALL into
His arms and find Him everything
you will ever need.*

ACKNOWLEDGMENTS

Behind this book there are people whose talents and efforts make the author appear far better than she really is.

To the three who know this story best, as it is, in part, their story, too:

Thank you to my mom, Trixie Mercer, who sacrificed behind the scenes and raised Mark and me with such extravagant love and laughter, we never got it until much later how little money we actually had! You're amazing!

To my brother, Mark Mercer, who, while I attempted to have a romantic moment with my high school boyfriend in the living room, intentionally ran past us in nothing but hiked-up "tighty whities", shouting, "See my fenders?" How did such a pesky little brother turn out to be my best friend and hero? You are the most wonderful brother a sister could have, and I love you, fenders and all.

And to my husband, John: how can a girl be so lucky as to have her very own chef, who stood at the stove creating delicious five star dinners while listening to my rough drafts and helping me shape these words? Thank you for the way you love me,

PROLOGUE

Perhaps you've stumbled upon this book and you're hurting, depressed, discouraged, or possibly even traumatized.

Maybe you're angry, have become cynical or have even lost hope because of painful circumstances you didn't sign up for.

Maybe you feel like you were on a joy ride when life's events took a sudden unexpected turn. You feel like you've been shoved out of a plane and are now falling through the air, out of control and headed for a terrible crash.

Maybe you've had one heartbreak after another and feel like you cannot take one more. Everything in you is screaming, "This was NOT supposed to happen to me!"

When we feel like we're falling, other thoughts may flood our minds as well. These thoughts might include:
"*My* God would never let (you fill in the blank) happen."
"I feel like I'm going under, but God will never give me more than I can handle, right?"
"I just don't deserve this."

Or perhaps your thoughts swing to the other side of the coin:

"Maybe God is getting back at me for some past sin."

If you've ever grappled with thoughts like these, know you're not alone. I'm glad you picked up this book. Those same thoughts have knocked on the door of my

heart and mind. And while I don't know everything you're feeling, I do have an idea of some of the things you may be experiencing.

We are either coming out of a storm, in the middle of a storm, or about to go into a storm. And I want you to be ready the next time a storm comes your way. And it will come.

Having gone through divorce, the death of my father by suicide and a few other personal tragedies, I know firsthand that when you go through loss so deep it changes your world, the pain seems to define you for a while. When those thoughts came knocking, I needed truth—not myths or hunches—to help me deal with my circumstances.

I've written this book for the person in a season of sorrow, whether through failing health, loss of a loved one, financial disaster or relationship problems. But this book is not just for the hurting. It's also for anyone who loves someone who is hurting and wants to know what to say to help comfort them.

This book is even for the person whose life is rosy at the moment. Why? Because it's wisely been said we are either coming out of a storm, in the middle of a storm, or about to go into a storm. And I want you to be ready the next time a storm comes your way. And it will come.

I believe our paths have crossed for a reason. I tread reverently and gently here, because I know that in the excruciating process of grief, it may take some time before you are ready to hear from others. But

With God by your side, it is possible to do more than just fall. You can "fall up." You can make it to the other side of grief stronger in your broken places.

may I share some encouraging news with you? I've learned that when heartbreak hits, with God by your side, it is possible to do more than just fall. You can "fall up." You can make it to the other side of grief stronger in your broken places.

In fact, over time, it's possible to move beyond "being stuck" and even to be used by God as a healing catalyst for others. Only God can heal a broken heart.

CHAPTER ONE

A Strange Dream

*"The Lord himself goes before you
and will be with you."*

- Deuteronomy 31:8

I am not a morning person.

One of my college roommates couldn't wait to greet the morning by throwing the blinds open with a sunny "Good morning, World!" I, on the other hand, like to ease into my day with a groan. And it's apparently true that opposites attract. My husband John is cheerfully up and at 'em at the first sign of daybreak, while I spend a few minutes each morning in denial—with a pillow over my head.

So you'll understand how unusual it was for me, one Fall morning in 2005, to wake up before daylight and jump out of bed with total exuberance. And although I was wide awake, I was confused about a dream I'd had that night.

At that point in time I was on staff in the music ministry of my church, and every Sunday my place was somewhere on the platform, either serving in the choir, in the vocal ensemble or at the piano. In my dream I was also in church. But instead of being in my usual place, I was standing with the congregation in the center of the first pew as our worship leader led the singing.

My exhilaration was more than I had ever experienced. I was so joyful that as we sang my hands extended straight up in praise. Something I never did. I didn't mind that others raised their hands in worship. It simply wasn't my style. In fact, the very thought of doing it made me feel uncomfortable and conspicuous. But in this dream, the incredible joy I felt trumped my usual reservations and I didn't care what others thought. I was compelled to express my highest and deepest praise.

I shared the dream with John. "It was a magnificent dream," I said, "but why was I was in the congregation and not on the platform? And why was I in the front center pew instead of on the side where we always sit during the sermon?" John agreed it was strange, but that dreams are often puzzling anyway.

One week later—to the day—I would know exactly what my dream meant.

CHAPTER TWO

Falling

"If at first you don't succeed…
then skydiving definitely isn't for you."

- Steven Wright

"For I am about to fall,
and my pain is ever with me."

- Psalm 38:17

I went skydiving the other day.

You may be asking, "Why would a sane person jump out of a perfectly good airplane?" For fun! For adventure! For lack of good sense!

I chose the recommended "tandem jump" since I was a first-timer. I would be fastened to an expert skydiver with a parachute.

It was all fun and games while I was on the ground, although my smile faded a bit when I inquired about landing instructions. The instructor's response? "Ah, don't worry…the ground will stop you."

Aren't you adorable? I thought to myself as I rolled my eyes.

We boarded the plane with plenty of laughing and joking. But the higher we ascended, the quieter I got. When the plane door opened at 14,000 feet, reality hit me like a freight train.

What the heck was I thinking? Exactly what about this

"kamikaze moment" did I think would be fun? CLOSE THAT DOOR! SOMEONE COULD FALL OUT! Oh, wait. That's the whole point.

Suddenly, the tandem jumpers in front of me slid to the open door and were gone...just like that! Immediately

my instructor—to whom I was tightly hooked—began nudging me forward from behind.

Instinctively, I pushed back.

Exactly what about this "kamikaze moment" did I think would be fun? CLOSE THAT DOOR! SOMEONE COULD FALL OUT! Oh, wait. That's the whole point.

My instructor pushed me forward again. This time more forcefully.

I wanted to talk about it. I wanted to review the instructions. Actually, I wanted out! And not the way out he was pushing me. *This was a bad idea,* I now thought. *Let's just land, have a cup of hot chocolate and watch the other idiots jump, okay?*

Nudging became shoving. I didn't like being fastened to him anymore. I didn't like where he was headed. Good grief, this was dangerous! Maybe I could reason with him, I thought as I dug my shoes into the floor of the plane.

But the engine's roar and the rush of air prohibited negotiation.

Talkin' time was ovah! It was time to jump.

I gave up resisting and the next moment I was hurtling through space and toward the ground at 120 mph!

Have you ever felt like that? Like you were falling? With absolutely no control?

One thing is certain. By God's design, at some point in time, we will all find ourselves FALLING. By that I mean we will be in a season when life's troubles are simply more than we can handle.

There are many ways we can find ourselves FALLING. What are you facing today?
- An ominous report from the doctor?
- A spouse who told you he'd love you forever but walked out for someone else, or for no reason at all?
- The slow, torturous decline of an elderly parent in the grip of Alzheimer's?
- A wayward son or daughter over whom you're wearing out your knees in prayer, but apparently to no avail?

In life's devastating, knee-knocking moments, we want to know…
- Where is God?

- What is He doing in my life?
- Why would a loving God allow this to happen to me?
- How can I remain steady and balanced in a season that threatens to derail the very core of my faith?
- Okay, forget "steady and balanced." How do I just get through this?

When I lost my father to suicide, I felt that, for all the world, I was falling. In the midst of gut-wrenching grief, I wanted God to use my suffering for His glory. The pain was more than I felt I could endure, but I desired more than anything to discover that all I'd been hearing, learning and talking about in church for the past 40-something years is true. And I'm here to tell you that IT IS TRUE.

One thing is certain. By God's design, at some point in time, we will all find ourselves FALLING.

Through God's grace, and without even realizing it, He led me through four steps. There was no apparent order to them, but I found myself constantly in one of these four postures during that agonizing time. And while there was no easy answer or quick fix to my grief, His leading me through these steps gradually brought me out of the pit.

I'd like to share with you those four practical steps you can use to deal with life when you feel like you're falling. There's no shortcut in life's most difficult moments, but God used these steps to lead me into healing, wholeness and a deeper understanding of His grace as I navigated the waters of a devastating sorrow. And He can and will do the same for you. I pray you will use them when you feel like you're

f

a

l

l

i

n

g.

CHAPTER THREE

Freefall

"The Lord upholds all those who fall...."

- Psalm 145:14

W hat do you wanna do?" "I don't know, what do you wanna do?" The age-old question of kids. "Is your dad at home?" my two best friends would ask. If the answer was "Yes," the instant reply was, "Let's go to your house!"

My dad was the fun dad who had silly nicknames for all my friends. The radio announcer with the FM voice acted as our very own Bert Parks, narrating and interviewing us with a cassette tape recorder, as we played dress-up in our homemade Miss America Pageant.

Years later, when I competed in the Miss Georgia Pageant, I received this treasure of a letter from him:
To My Precious Daughter,
Tonight the judges will decree who (in their fallible opinion) is the new Miss Georgia.
I pray it is you! If it is not, however, know that in my heart and mind
you long ago captured the title of Miss Universe.
I shall pray for you, not so much that you shall win, but that you will know the joy of having striven.
All my love, Dad

Now, my Aunt Wee Wee told it a little more like it was.

Dear Connie,
You will not be the prettiest.
But darlin' you will be the sweetest.

Thanks, Aunt Wee Wee. Just what I was aiming for.

Back to the story.

He was the fun dad.

But he also had another side. He also struggled with major depressive episodes and, consequently, wrestled with his own sense of worth, value, acceptance, belonging and feeling loved. In an effort to numb the intense pain of those unmet emotional needs, he turned to alcohol. Over time, he became enslaved. An alcoholic. Alcoholism and the issues that come with it eventually contributed to my parents' divorce.

Even so, to meet him was to love him. Handsome, articulate and winsome, he was blessed with a quick wit and a gift for words.

His thoughtfulness was exemplified in the following scenario. Even though my parents divorced, for the next 30 years, he never failed to send my mom a Mother's Day card thanking her for being the mother of his children, and for how she raised and nurtured them.

Then at age 70, he did a remarkable thing. He went to rehab, completed the program, joined Alcoholics Anonymous and had wonderful success. Later, totally unrelated to his addiction, he became ill and was hospitalized. When I saw him, I called John. "I think he needs to live with us." "Of course," was John's instant reply.

And so our lives changed overnight—from being just the two of us to lunches at the local cafeteria, wading through Medicare and way too much Scrabble! Sitting at the dining room table after dinner, studying the Scrabble board, Dad would say, "I think we all agree that the word *smelt* refers to the extraction of iron for ore." As if we really knew. And then he would make a winning move. What? The only *smelt* I knew about had to do with my husband's tennis shoes that I wouldn't allow in our closet. "Dad, that's not a word. You can't use that." But sure enough, we'd look it up and find it was indeed a word! He was the undisputed Scrabble champion!

Many nights I walked in the back door to find John and my dad staring wide-eyed at the TV with the entranced look that told me they were watching *Band of Brothers*, the World War II docudrama. I loved eavesdropping from the kitchen as they swapped war stories. Didn't matter which war. Civil War, World War II, Vietnam…the discussion was always lively.

My dad had been in bars most nights when I was growing up. Later, when my parents divorced, our relationship was congenial, but distant. Now, our daily lives became wonderfully entwined: cooking together, sharing meals, taking strolls together, going to the doctor together and going to church together. Talk about a one-eighty!

As my dad recuperated, we began to talk of him getting his own place in our town. He was excited about the prospect and we began searching. Before long, we found the perfect place—a brand new condominium. My brother Mark handled the sweaty, backbreaking task of moving our dad's furniture while I had the easy part of helping to decide where pictures should be hung and knickknacks should be placed. Together, we all had a great time.

Looking back, I realize now that he needed to be with people—not living alone.

Sometimes in low moments, Dad would remind me of past failures that lurked in his mind. Broken promises, missed recitals and swim meets, loud and angry words spewed out under the influence of alcohol. Doors slamming and pictures crashing to the floor. Tires screeching out of the driveway. Absent for days at a time. I remember getting sick at school on more than one occasion, wondering where my father was and if he was okay.

Although he had mellowed through the years and was now walking a life of sobriety, the ghosts still haunted him and he would again beg my forgiveness. "That's over, Dad," I would remind him. "You are forgiven, by God and by me. It's a brand new day. Let's enjoy it."

He would sadly smile and nod, but the pain of past regrets was still evident in his eyes.

One day we were in the car together on the way to the grocery store. Gazing out the window, he said softly, and with a little bit of a chuckle, "Sometimes I think it'd be better for everybody if this ol' man just went on to heaven." The statement concerned me, but not too much. Caught off guard, I replied awkwardly, "Oh, now… that's not true."

When people talk of ending their lives, even in euphemistic terms, don't take it lightly. It means they are considering it.

If someone ever says that to you, no matter how quietly or nonchalantly, pull over and stop the car. Put the newspaper down. Turn the TV or computer off. Stop whatever you are doing. Look deeply into his eyes. Take his hands in yours. Tell him how much he means to you and that your life would *not* be better off without him. When people talk of ending their lives, even in euphemistic terms, don't take it lightly. It means they are considering it.

After years of not having a checkbook, my dad opened an account and asked me to help him with it. Things were going fine. He kept up with his checkbook to the penny. Since my name was jointly on the account, I checked in with him on a monthly basis. On a Thursday, I asked him if we could go over his monthly statement. He didn't want to. I pressed. Finally, he handed it over.

"Dad, there's a check entry missing."

"Really?" he asked.

"Do you remember the check you wrote that's missing?" I asked.

"Hmmm....no." he replied, with a furrowed brow, as if it was a mystery to him, too.

"Don't worry, I'll call the bank," I assured him.

I returned to my office, made the call and learned that the missing check was paid to a title pawn company. It was the same company that John and I had paid off for him three months earlier.

I drove to my dad's place, knocked on the door and, finding it unlocked, opened the door. "Dad?" I called. He came around the corner. "Dad, you took another loan out with the title pawn shop. Their interest is enormously high," I fussed. "If you need money, let us know. But please don't do that again."

Shame and anger disfigured his face. "Did you knock before you came in?"

"Yes, I did. You must not have heard me."

He walked out of the kitchen, leaving me standing there.

"I love you, Dad. Dad?"

No response. I let myself out.

The next day, Friday, I attended a conference and was struck by the speaker's words: "Listen. Bad things happen. And when they do, that is the time to put into practice what you've been talking about in church all these years."

I thought about calling my dad, but thought he might want a little space since our conversation the day before. Still, I picked up my cell phone, started to dial his number, but put the phone back in my purse instead.

On Saturday evening, I was part of a musical concert. Dad and John had planned to attend the concert together, but we hadn't heard from him. Throughout the day, I called and left a few messages reminding him of the concert, saying how much we hoped he would join us. Uneasiness began to hover over me. Since he had just moved into his new home we wanted to give him a bit of independence. Not wanting to intrude, we chose not to drop in on him unannounced and instead waited for him to return our calls. But he didn't.

Just before the concert, I chatted with Rob, a dear friend and fellow musician. The conversation turned to the goodness of God. Seemingly out of the blue he said, "When my brother committed suicide, God told me that I needed to put that event in a file in my mind and label it 'Will Never Make Sense in this Life' and shut the drawer. I could go crazy trying to analyze it and figure it all out, but the truth is God holds that file for me." He went on to explain that his healing had come from leaving that terrible mystery with our sovereign, loving God. I replied to Rob, "I'm so glad God did that for you." As the lights dimmed and the concert began, I turned around to take my place at the keyboard and thought, "That was a strange and random conversation."

On Sunday morning, John and I listened to the sermon titled "Caring for Others." Since moving to our town, Dad was always at church. But not today. Over lunch, we discussed the sermon and asked ourselves who we knew that needed a tangible reminder of the love of Christ. Little did we know that in the next hour we would find ourselves in the deepest need of care we had ever experienced. After several unreturned phone messages, our nagging concern had grown. So the last message we left my dad said we were on our way over.

As John and I drove into his new neighborhood, we saw his car at the end of the road. "What's Dad's car doing there?" we asked each other. The car faced us as we slowly cruised toward it. As we got closer to the car I saw my father's left leg sprawled behind the rear tire. Instinctively I grabbed the phone, thinking he'd had a heart attack or stroke. It was only as we rolled forward and I saw the shotgun that I realized the truth: my father had taken his own life.

John cried, "Don't look, Sugar, don't look!" But I had already seen enough for a lifetime, an image that is forever seared into my brain. I heard my husband sobbing into the phone with a 911 operator, "My father-in-law shot himself. Please send help!"

The checkbook incident from Thursday had left a worrisome weight on my heart since it happened. Now the weight became a crushing boulder. Because, obviously, it had bothered my dad, too.

I reached into the backseat for John's Bible and began to thumb through the pages, keeping my head turned the other way. "Lord, this can't be happening! I'm running into Your arms, Jesus. You're in charge of my good times and bad. I know that you are here with me in this moment. Help me. By Your grace, help me!"

In a providential turn of events, I flipped open God's Word and it spoke to me in that very moment with what I needed: *Whom have I in heaven but You? And earth has nothing I desire besides you. My flesh and my heart may fail, but God is the strength of my heart and my portion forever (Psalm 73:25, 26).*

The speaker's challenge from Friday flooded my mind. *Bad things will happen. When they do, that's the time to put into practice what you've been talking about in church all these years.*

The speaker's challenge from Friday flooded my mind. "Bad things will happen. When they do, that's the time to put into practice what you've talking about in church all these years."

The memory of my friend's words from the night before about his brother's suicide surrounded me like a cloak. Even in the middle of nauseating grief, I knew God had gone before me, preparing me for this moment. I saw clearly that the past five months with my father had been an extraordinary gift from God, restoring to me the years the locusts had eaten (Joel 2:25).

We called our friend Mac and he was there in minutes. As he held me, he whispered, "You know your daddy's in heaven."

"Yes, he is."

There had been many years of prayer and concern for my dad's eternal destiny, and graciously the Lord had given me, through recent conversations with my father, assurance of his salvation. I had shared this with Mac and he reminded me of it now. Even in the middle of this devastating sorrow, it was awe-inspiring to know that my father was free of his burden of depression and the pull of alcohol.

A note was found on the passenger seat of Dad's car:

To my dearest family,
My deepest thanks to you for all you have
attempted on my behalf.
I am simply unworthy. I can never be
what is expected of me.
The worn-out corpse perishes but the love
remains forever…
Dad

This brilliant, winsome man took his own life. In this ultimate act of selfishness, he left behind broken hearts, unanswered questions and a storm of ambivalent emotions for those who loved him.

I called my mother. Although my parents had been divorced many years, there had remained a type of love between them, always wanting the best for each other and for my brother Mark and me. I knew my mom was out of town on a girls' trip. When I told her what had happened, I heard her cry – something I have rarely heard my strong mom do. And then she said she would be home as soon as possible.

Next I needed to call Mark. But that was easier said than done. A flight engineer, he had just touched down in Qatar for his next 90-day tour of duty flying over Iraq and Afghanistan. The only way to get a message to him was through his wife. As soon as he got the news, he caught a return flight home.

We asked Mac to speak at the funeral, knowing that he would deal head on with, not hide from, the issue of suicide.

As word traveled and friends began to arrive at the condo, I explained as best I could what had happened. I remember sitting, nodding and studying the carpet between my flip flops as friends struggled with what to say. No tears came. I called other family members to tell them, heard their anguished moans and sobs, but still did not cry. The rest of the day was spent answering calls, contacting the funeral home and taking care of a mountain of details.

Later that night, John and I got ready for bed. I brushed my teeth. I washed my face. Like every other night. But this night, as I looked into the mirror, I saw my father's resemblance in my face. Grief began to rise in my throat and a sudden tsunami of sorrow slammed into my soul as I imagined what my father must have experienced in the hours and moments that led to his end. I heard myself wail, groan and sob with sounds I didn't recognize as mine. As John held me, I felt that my very skin hurt. The thought of my dad's agony was too much to comprehend.

My freefall of grief had begun.

CHAPTER FOUR

F – Focus

"Let us fix our eyes on Jesus...."

- Hebrews 12:2

"You will keep in perfect peace him whose mind is steadfast, because he trusts in You."

- Isaiah 26:3

I excitedly entered the hangar where the skydivers were gathering. After signing my life away, I was introduced to my instructor. Each skydiver was assigned to his own personal instructor, to whom he would be fastened. But first, it was Jump School.

The place was busier and louder than Best Buy on Christmas Eve. I found myself surrounded with larger than life videos of skydivers on big screens accompanied by the loud thumping bass lines of Van Halen and the Pointer Sisters. (Can you say "JUMP?") The room was filled to capacity with groups of two: one instructor and one student. All over the room, instructors were explaining the correct way to jump out of a plane.

My private lesson began. "We'll exit the plane with arms folded across the chest. When I push you forward, don't hesitate. Arch your back and slightly bend your knees. When I tap your shoulders, spread both arms out for the rest of the way down. Remember to smile. It'll tighten your cheeks so they won't flap as much."

I hung on my expert instructor's every word as I quickly realized that my life was literally in his hands. But I couldn't help overhearing other instructors who were explaining different techniques to their students. All around me I heard snatches of directions from other instructors. I tried to keep my attention on my instructor but I kept getting distracted. *Why aren't all the instructors giving the same instructions?* I wondered. As if reading my mind, he got really close to my face and said these words: "You'll hear other instructors giving directions to their partners. I am your partner. I do things differently than them. Focus on me only, listen to me only and you'll be fine."

I was all ears.

Sometimes life can be like Jump School. We have a lot of distractions trying to capture our attention . . . especially when we're going through a tough time. But the choice of where we focus our attention is totally up to us. We are the only person who can make that decision.

We can choose to believe lies over truth and passively travel the path of least resistance. Or we can work hard to keep our focus on truth, and fight back against those lies.

What you and I choose to focus our thoughts on has a direct impact on how we feel. And how we feel greatly influences what we do. "For as he thinketh in his heart, so is he" (Proverbs 23:7 KJV). Carrying that forward, what we do then impacts how we feel. And the cycle continues. I've heard many hurting people say they can't help their feelings. That's true, but feelings are determined by thoughts—and we can choose what we think about.

We can choose to believe lies over truth and passively travel the path of least resistance. Or we can work hard to keep our focus on truth, and fight back against those lies.

The coroner's report says that my father died of a self-inflicted gunshot wound. But there was another cause of death that happened first: he died from listening to the wrong voice. I was astonished at how believing lies and focusing on them could have such a catastrophic impact on a life.

Yet now the same voice threatened me. Sitting at traffic lights, standing in the shower and wandering the house in the middle of sleepless nights, I heard the insidious whispers of the enemy:

What must it have been like for your dad in those terrible last moments? Your poor, precious dad. But then, how could he have done this to you and everyone else who loved him? How dare he leave in such a selfish manner? If you had been there, you could've stopped him. If only you had been there. (Lather. Rinse. Repeat.)

Bouncing like a ping pong ball in a Bermuda triangle between pity for my father, then anger toward him, then guilt for not having been there, I felt a gravitational pull toward a very black sorrow.

The coroner's report says that my father died of a self-inflicted gunshot wound. But there was another cause of death that happened first: he died from listening to the wrong voice.

Having seen the devastating power of a lie in my father's life, I knew it was crucial that I focus on TRUTH instead. But I needed a TRUE picture of my circumstances, not just a re-play of my emotions. I knew it wouldn't be easy, I knew it would be a process and I knew I would need God's help.

So I asked God to help me recognize the lies, and I started filling my mind with His TRUTH. Day by day, hour by hour and sometimes even minute by minute, as if my life depended on it, I began to proactively replace the lies that threatened to destroy me with corresponding truths from God's Word.

Here are some of the ways I did that.

Focus on Finding Joy

Since the New Testament believers were no strangers to trials and suffering, I decided that would be a great place to find scripture verses I could use to replace the lies that were trying to overwhelm me and help me discover joy on this journey.

What I found is that there is encouragement, and even a commandment, to pursue —to focus on—joy in the middle of our painful circumstances.

Here are some examples of verses I meditated on daily:
- "Dear friends, do not be surprised at the painful trial you are suffering, as though something strange were happening to you" (1 Peter 4:12).
- "Blessed are you when people...persecute you...*Rejoice and be glad*, because great is your reward in heaven" (Matthew 5:11-12).
- "The apostles left...*rejoicing* because they had been counted worthy of suffering disgrace for the Name" (Acts 5:41).
- "We also *rejoice* in our sufferings, because we know that suffering produces perseverance..." (Romans 5:3).
- "*Consider it pure joy*, my brothers, whenever you face trials of many kinds, because you know that the testing of your faith develops perseverance" (James 1:2-3).
- "Remember those earlier days after you had received the light, when you stood your ground

in a great contest in the face of suffering. Sometimes you were publicly exposed to insult and persecution; at other times you stood side by side with those who were so treated. You sympathized with those in prison and *joyfully* accepted the confiscation of your property, because you knew that you yourselves had better and lasting possessions" (Hebrews 10:32-34).

- "So do not throw away your confidence; it will be richly rewarded. You need to persevere so that when you have done the will of God, you will receive what he has promised" (Hebrews 10:35).

And the best example I find is Jesus, "who for the *joy* set before him endured the cross" (Hebrews 12:2).

What gave these New Testament believers joy in the middle of hardship, disappointment and persecution? Not their circumstances, but the good things happening behind the scenes. Being transformed into the likeness of Christ, developing the muscle of perseverance, and investing in the eternal rewards they knew were waiting for them.

What could have given Jesus the determination and sustaining power to endure the awful suffering of the cross? Not the experience of humiliation and suffering itself, but what He knew the outcome would be—our salvation and His Father's pleasure.

Focus on Fighting for Joy by Preaching to Yourself

The writings of John Piper and Martyn Lloyd-Jones have been transformational in my journey. They both encourage us to "preach to yourself." Why? Because we can be certain that the devil never stops preaching to us! If we simply go on "default" setting, the lies of the enemy are always there to pull us down into depression, doubt, hatred, and self-pity.

Lloyd-Jones, in his book *Spiritual Depression: Its Causes and Cures*, discusses Psalm 42:5: "Why are you downcast, O my soul? Why so disturbed within me? Put your hope in God, for I will yet praise Him, my Savior and my God."

Have you realized that most of your unhappiness in life is due to the fact that you are listening to yourself instead of talking to yourself? Take those thoughts that come to you the moment you wake up in the morning. You have not originated them but they are talking to you, they bring back the problems of yesterday, etc. Somebody is talking. Who is talking to you? Your self is talking to you. Now this man's treat {in Psalm 42} was this: instead of allowing this self to talk to him, he starts talking to himself. "Why are thou cast down, O my soul?" he asks. His soul had been depressing him, crushing him. So he stands up and says, "Self, listen for a moment, I will speak to you."[1]

John Piper refers to Lloyd-Jones' writing as a profound lesson, saying,

> Far too many Christians are passive in their fight for joy. They tell me about their condition of joyless-ness, and I ask about the kinds of strategies they have pursued to defeat this enemy, and they give the impression that they are a helpless victim.... Well, God does not mean for us to be passive. He means for us to fight the fight of faith – the fight for joy. And the central strategy is to preach the gospel to yourself. This is war. Satan is preaching for sure. If we remain passive we surrender the field to him.[2]

We don't seem to have any trouble understanding this principle when it comes to our physical body.

If I asked you, "Did you get up early, go the gym and work out this morning...by accident?" You would chuckle at the ridiculousness of it and reply, "Of course not."

You and I know that any discipline in life, whether it's physical exercise, saving money or quitting smoking requires us to, as Nike says, "Just Do It." Yet we seem to forget that where our emotions are concerned, we can't just put them on autopilot. We have to maintain discipline in that area of our life, too.

Is it wrong to have discouraging, distressing and even hopeless thoughts? No. Even Jesus experienced these thoughts. In the Garden of Gethsemane, we see the deep, troubling thoughts of our Savior: "He took Peter and the two sons of Zebedee along with him, and he began to be sorrowful and troubled. Then he said to them, 'My soul is overwhelmed with sorrow to the point to death'" (Matthew 26:37-38). Since Jesus was sinless, then his emotions were appropriate for the moment he was enduring. So understand I'm not asking you to "drum up" some joy. Instead, we need to realize the danger of allowing despondent thoughts to fester.

Piper explains it this way:

> The first shockwaves of the blast of despondency are not the sin. The sin is in not turning on the air-raid siren, and not heading for the bomb shelters, and not deploying the antiaircraft weapons. If Satan drops a bomb on your peace, and you don't make ready for war, people are going to wonder whose side you're on. It's just the same with Jesus. The first shockwaves of despondency that he feels because of the assaults of temptation are not sin. But no one knew better than Jesus how quickly they can become sin, if they are not counterattacked immediately. You cannot read Matthew 26:36-39 and come away saying, 'Despondency's not so bad, because Jesus had it in Gethsemane and he's sinless.' Instead, what you come away with is an impression of how earnestly he fought off the unbelief of despondency. How much more should we![3]

Focus on God's Truth

It's important that we discipline ourselves to fill our hearts and our minds with truth. To preach to ourselves.

We don't naturally always think beautiful, glorious, uplifting thoughts. Maybe that's why we are reminded in Philippians 4:8, "...whatever is true, whatever is noble, whatever is right, whatever is pure, whatever is lovely, whatever is admirable – if anything is excellent or praiseworthy – think about such things."

I know you're thinking you already know this, but hear me out. When we're in a period of darkness and it doesn't seem to be going away, the soil of our heart is so soft that anything can be planted in it. Not only truth... but also lies. Because of that fact, it's important that we discipline ourselves to fill our hearts and our minds with truth. To preach to ourselves.

So what should we focus on when we have such painful memories, whether it happened 40 years ago or day before yesterday? How do we get a clearer picture of the event? We can ask God to give us a glimpse of the event from His perspective. We can ask Him to adjust our spiritual vision.

Then we can run the hurtful memory through the grid of Philippians 4:8.

For many years, I secretly rolled my eyes at Philippians 4:8 "…whatever is true, whatever is noble, whatever is right, whatever is pure, whatever is lovely, whatever is admirable, if anything is excellent or praiseworthy – think about such things." This verse always reminded me of the song "My Favorite Things" from *The Sound of Music*. In the middle of my gut-wrenching pain, is the Bible encouraging me to think about *my* favorite things?

Really?!?

The verse seemed like a naïve diversion from real life pain. No matter how I focused on strolling on the beach at sunset, it didn't change the fact that my father took his life. Remembering favorite hikes through the woods may give me a warm fuzzy for a moment, but then I have to return to real life and all its problems. And sure, there are plenty of true, pure and lovely things to think about. But at the end of the day, my dad was still dead.

Then one day the Lord gave me a different perspective. He wasn't telling me to think Pollyanna thoughts just for the sake of diverting my attention *from* my father's suicide. God was encouraging me to explore with Him what might be true, noble, lovely, admirable, excellent and praiseworthy *about* my father's suicide.

As strange as it may sound, when I began to consider my situation in the context of this verse, the crushing

When I began to consider my situation in the context of this verse, the crushing weight in my chest slowly began to subside and my first glimpse of healing began.

weight in my chest slowly began to subside and my first glimpse of healing began.

At first glance, you may find it difficult to find the true, noble and lovely things about your situation. But keep looking. Here's how this worked for me regarding my dad.

Focus on whatever is true:

My dad was broken and flawed. That's true. But it's also true that he's not anymore. I choose to picture my father—not in the confused, tormented state he was in just before he died—but as the whole, healthy father he is now. God tells us in Revelation 21:4 that "He will wipe every tear from their eyes. There will be no more death or mourning or crying or pain, for the old order of things has passed away."

I also focused on the truth that even in the middle of the darkness that overwhelmed my dad, God's light was shining in his soul. I will be eternally grateful because I learned just weeks before his death that my dad's trust was in the Lord Jesus Christ! It may have been faith the size of a mustard seed and it may have come late in life, but God assures me that it is enough (Matthew 17:20, Luke 23:42-43).

Focus on whatever is noble (good, honorable):

God didn't forget about me. He didn't let me fall through the cracks. He wasn't busy answering someone else's prayer while mine got lost in the paperwork of Heaven.

His Word assures me that "All the days ordained for me were written in [His] book before one of them came to be" (Psalm 139:16). "[He] can do all things. No plan of [His] can be thwarted" (Job 42:2). His plans for me are good, even when it doesn't look like it from where I'm sitting (Jeremiah 29:11). He assures me that He is "close to the brokenhearted and saves those who are crushed in spirit" (Psalm 34:18).

Satan loves to taunt us with regrets of the past. I know that Satan set out to destroy me with the "if onlys." "If only" I'd followed my hunch and gone to my dad's home sooner. In the five months he lived in my town, that Friday was the first day I didn't see him. If only, if only, if only. The regrets are always there. And if I choose to focus on them, they're ready to destroy me. Or I can choose to see them for what they are: LIES.

Are you being held captive by the "if onlys?" Are you a prisoner of past experiences? Here's what I mean: "Boy, those were the good old days. When I was single.

Before I had kids. Before I made that wrong choice. When I still had my youth. If only I could go back and have a do-over." Are you missing out on what God has for you today because you're consumed with yesterday?

Are you being held captive by the "if onlys"? Instead of looking back and wishing something had gone differently or regretting that something is over, don't miss out on what He is doing now.

In the middle of whatever you're going through, you can find something to praise Him for. Instead of looking back and wishing something had gone differently or regretting that something is over, don't miss out on what He is doing right now.

I love what God says in Isaiah 43:18-19: "Forget the former things; do not dwell on the past. See, I am doing a new thing! Now it springs up; do you not perceive it?" Are you held captive by your past experience, whether good or bad? Don't let it keep you from experiencing the new work God is doing in your life right now. Yes, right now, in the middle of your current situation.

The apostle Paul says, "We demolish arguments and every pretension that sets itself up against the knowledge of God, and we take captive every thought to make it obedient to Christ" (2 Corinthians 10:5).

How do we put that verse into practice? We can literally say to a thought that knocks on the door to our brain, "Are you true? Are you beneficial? Are you necessary?" And if the answer to any one of those three questions is no, then we don't answer the door. We choose to walk away from the lie and all the negativity that could result in our life if we let it in.

If we are to find any contentment or peace in the midst of adversity, it is vital that we accept our situation as being intentionally allowed into our lives by a loving and personal God.

Andrew Murray, author of *Abide in Christ*, gave the following advice for those who are in the trials of life:

> *In the time of trouble, say:*
> 1. *God has brought me here. It is by His will that I am in this place. In that I will rest.*
> 2. *He will keep me here in His love and give me grace in this trial to behave as His child.*
> 3. *He will make the trial a blessing, teaching me lessons He intends me to learn, and working in me the grace He means to bestow.*
> 4. *In His good time He can bring me out again. How and when, only He knows.*
>
> *Therefore, say, "I am here by God's appointment, in His keeping, under His training and for His time."*[4]

God is sovereign. He is the God of our past, our present and our future. We can trust Him to take care of our yesterdays as much as our tomorrows. It is such a comfort to live free of the "if onlys!"

God is sovereign. He is the God of our past, present and future. We can trust Him to take care of our yesterdays as much as our tomorrows.

Focus on whatever is pure:

God bought and paid for me with the precious blood of His own dear Son. I am of infinite worth to Him. He loves me with a pure love.

Because Satan knows how much I'm worth to the Father, he tries his best to destroy me. One of his favorite methods is to whisper lies to me about myself and about my situation until I believe them and act them out.

Instead, I choose to believe and focus on what *God* says about me and how much He loves me.

Focus on whatever is lovely (pleasing):

To realize that I don't have to have it all figured out pleases me very much. How wonderful it is to know that God holds life's mysteries for us. "The secret things belong to the Lord our God" (Deuteronomy 29:29). His thoughts are not my thoughts…they are higher than mine (Isaiah 55:8-9) and one day I'll understand fully and clearly (1 Corinthians 13:12).

Another pleasant thought I choose to focus on sometimes is the reunion my dad and I will have in Heaven one day.

One day I'll reach Heaven, and my dad will be waiting for me. Not in the stooped, broken way a lifetime of poor choices had made him as he left this earth. Oh no! He'll be standing tall, with a bouquet of heavenly flowers in his hand. He'll scoop me up into his arms, and after a moment of joyful tears I'll say something like, "You old rascal! What were you thinking?" In his famous FM radio voice he'll reply with a smile, "Not the smartest thing I ever did."

And do you know what will happen next?

We'll laugh!

We'll pick right up where we left off, except our relationship will be void of trials and tears. It will be full of new beginnings. Why? Because that is our great God. We'll laugh and rejoice because for the first time we'll both see clearly with the mind of Christ all the wonderful things God did behind the scenes of our suffering on earth.

Focus on whatever is admirable, excellent, or praise-worthy:

Through this tragic event, God has birthed in me a desire to help bring comfort to others with what

He's done for me "...[He] comforts us in all our troubles, so that we can comfort those in any trouble with the comfort we ourselves have received from God" (2 Corinthians 1:4).

Our way out of the darkness is to choose to believe God more than we believe ourselves. To believe His voice of truth.

And that one outcome is worth praising Him.

In God's providence, great love and mercy, the very week my dad died, I heard a song for the first time. The song was "The Voice of Truth" by Casting Crowns and the lyrics were a godsend to me. The song talks about *choosing* to listen and *choosing* to believe the voice of truth instead of any of the other voices that are trying to capture our attention.

I've learned that our human perspective of life's events is simply not accurate and can't be trusted. What God says about you and me is the truth. Our way out of the darkness is to choose to believe God more than we believe ourselves. To believe His voice of truth.

Every regret, every seemingly wrong turn He will redeem and make into something precious. That's His business...He loves to do it! The great men and women of the Bible were extraordinarily used of God, not because they were perfect, but because they trusted God with their hopes, sorrows, questions, sins and imperfections. They believed God could do what He said He could do.

Focusing on the right things takes discipline. But it's worth all the hard work. Stop gulping down the devil's poisonous lies. Guard your mind with the Truth and keep it focused there.

Take Time to Reflect:

1. The Bible tells us that God is sovereign over our yesterdays, our todays and our tomorrows. How would your outlook change if you fully believed and focused on this truth?

2. God's Word promises that He is always doing a good thing, even in the middle of circumstances we don't fully understand. How could this truth help you in your situation?

3. What self-defeating thoughts run through your mind when you remember painful events in your life? What insights and perspective could you gain by asking the following questions about those thoughts?
- Is it true?
- Is it beneficial?
- Is it necessary?

4. Pass your painful event through the grid of Philippians 4:8 to direct your thoughts and gain a clearer understanding of that memory. Invite God to help you reframe your painful event by writing about it as you focus on:
- Whatever is true:
- Whatever is noble (good, honorable):
- Whatever is right:
- Whatever is pure:
- Whatever is lovely (pleasing):
- Whatever is admirable, excellent, or praiseworthy:

CHAPTER FIVE

A — Admit

"When I said, 'My foot is slipping,'
Your unfailing love, O Lord, supported me."

- Psalm 94:18

The young, 6'3" cocky fellow smirked as he watched me suit up. It was evident by the smug look on his face that he thought someone like me was out of place. After all, skydiving was for cool dudes, not middle-aged women. He swaggered over my way. "Let me guess. First time?" he asked with a chuckle.

"Yep. How about you?"

"Yeah," he replied with a Barney Fife kind of snort. "But this is no big deal. I'm the adventurous sort."

Then why are you doing the tandem jump? Why don't you just do the big boy jump by yourself? I wanted to ask, but didn't.

He was full of jokes. "Remember, you don't need a parachute to skydive. You just need one to do it again."

"You're cute. *Not really,*" I thought.

As our plane ascended and the door opened, however, his smile began to fade and his face began to blanch. Even behind his goggles, I could see the raw fear growing in his eyes. In only a matter of minutes, I witnessed his transformation from confidence to anxiety to full-blown panic. As his instructor began prodding him forward from behind, I heard this grown man scream like a girl, "I CAN'T DO THIS!"

Have you ever felt that way? That your life's current situation is more than you can handle?

When we can admit to God—and to ourselves—our true feelings about what life has handed us, we'll begin to see the light at the end of the tunnel.

When we can admit to God—and to ourselves—our true feelings about what life has handed us, we'll begin to see the light at the end of the tunnel.

Admit to God that it's more than you can handle.

A friend of yours describes one of these atrocious scenarios:

- Out of the blue, her spouse leaves.
- Or her teenage daughter is missing.
- An aging mother doesn't recognize her loving daughter.
- A surefire investment goes south, wiping out decades of hard-earned savings.
- The oncology report is not what was prayed for and the blue-eyed, four-year-old light of her life is fading away.

Wow! Life hurts.

But then your friend summarizes her gut-wrenching tale with these famous words: "I feel like I'm going under, but I know God will never give me more than I can handle." If her story is told in a church setting, heads nod and affirmative "amens" are heard around the room.

How many times have we heard it? Or said it? "God will never give you more than you can handle." But there's a problem with that wildly popular statement. It isn't biblical. And, unfortunately, the myth that God will "never give you more than you can handle" contributes to many people feeling there's something wrong with *them* when the heartaches pile up and they have difficulty handling them.

The myth that God will "never give you more than you can handle" contributes to many people feeling there's something wrong with them when heartaches pile up and they have difficulty handling them.

Like the cocky young man in the plane with me, we sometimes actually think we can handle our challenges on our own. And often we say to the Lord, "I'm good. I've got this. No problem. I've got it covered." But pretty soon, the plane door opens and before you can say "GERONIMO!" we're singing the same tune as the psalmist who said, "Troubles without number surround me" (Psalm 40:12).

And there's this from King David, the *man after God's own heart*: "Save me, O God, for the waters have come up to my neck. I sink in the miry depths, where there is no foothold. I have come into the deep waters; the floods engulf me. I am worn out calling for help; my throat is parched. My eyes fail, looking for my God" (Psalm 69:1-3).

Yes, there is a verse that says we will never be *tempted* beyond what we can bear (1 Cor. 10:13), but this is referring to temptation, not trials. The Bible makes it clear that God did indeed give some of his choice servants more than they could endure. Consider the Apostle Paul's report: "We do not want you to be uninformed, brothers, about the hardships we suffered in the province of Asia. We were under great pressure, *far beyond our ability to endure*, so that we despaired even of life. Indeed, in our hearts we felt the sentence of death. But this happened, that we might rely not on ourselves, but on God, who raises the dead" (2 Corinthians 1:8-9; italics mine).

We can take great comfort in knowing that our gracious God has made sure the Bible includes stories of saints who found themselves in over their heads, their back against the wall, knowing that their situation was more than they could handle.

If you think you can't handle your problems, congratulations! You're right! If you could handle them, who would get the glory? You. God leads us into desert-like situations so He alone can be our sufficiency. Then the glory is all His.

We also need to admit to God that we're angry.

Lisa Hellier's compelling story, her "Untestimony" as she calls it, is that of a good girl who did all the right things. "I was full up of good deeds!" says Lisa. Good grades, never in trouble. In Sunday School, she knew all the answers and gave them loudly, clearly and before anyone else did. She sang in the youth choir and spoke on Youth Sunday.

In college, even in her "going wild" she did it oh so respectfully. "Wild" with church attendance, "wild" with involvement in Christian organizations, "wild" with helping the less fortunate while all the hungover college kids slept in.

She married a good boy...a fourth-generation Presbyterian with a letter from John Wesley to an ancestor who wrote Bible commentaries. "Sheesh. We had heritage coming out our wazoo!" said Lisa. After she married, she led Bible studies and played piano for church. She and her husband were part-time youth ministers. Are you impressed yet???

But instead of the good life she expected in return for all these good deeds, her first son was born with a one-in-a-million genetic defect, Severe Combined Immune Deficiency. (Picture the Bubble Boy.) Even while in the hospital with her baby, she was convinced that this was nothing but a test for her to pass. "I witnessed, I shared the gospel, I prayed with and for others in the hospital and I promised God I would not watch another soap opera in my life if James could live. If I thought there was a ticket to punch, I was getting it punched."

But despite two years of doctor visits, numerous hospitalizations and earnest prayers, James died in her arms. Nothing could have prepared Lisa for such a tragedy.

The result? A cold, hard anger. An anger first directed at God that then spilled over onto anyone in her path. No one could comfort her to her satisfaction. Efforts by family or friends to reach out to her were rejected. No one could do anything right as far as she was concerned.

Lisa remembers waking up every morning consumed with anger. "I had done my part and God had not done His. I deserved better. He had not treated me as I deserved." But even though she was furious with God, she still wrestled with Him, telling Him the awful truth of her deep fury regarding the death of her son. God had not measured up to her standards.

Then a slow dawn began for Lisa as she read the book of Romans. She started to get a picture of the ways *she* had not measured up to *God's* standard. Then in Ezra 9:13 she read that God does not treat us like we deserve.

New insight came as Lisa reflected on the kindnesses of God: the gift of being able to adopt a child one year later. The blessing that her husband stayed with her during her anger. Friends who continued to pray for and reach out in compassion to Lisa even while they couldn't seem to get anything right in her eyes.

"It was then that I began to see that, indeed, God had not treated me like I deserved. Instead, He had been merciful to me." Lisa explains that painful circumstances are the times when we are

"It was then that I began to see that, indeed, God had not treated me like I deserved. Instead, He had been merciful to me."
— Lisa Hellier

most tempted to be offended with God. "It's wonderful that, in spite of my sinfulness, God, through Christ, has chosen to NEVER hold a grudge against me." (2 Corinthians 5:19). Her anger started to lose steam.

"I thought I had a right to be angry," she continues. "But it was only when I gave up my rights to the Lord's right over my life that I began to be restored. It was when I quit being angry with God that I was able to thank Him, not only for James' life, but even for his death. You see, through his death, the Lord showed me Himself in the most real way possible."

Lisa explains that before James' death, God was only a god of her construct. Maybe you've been there, too, while struggling to comprehend a life-shattering event?

"*My* God would never let my baby die."
"*My* God would never let an earthquake take the lives of so many."
"*My* God would never let (you fill in the blank) happen."

Yet, here's the problem. They are referring to *their* god, not the true God.

In response to similar statements after the Sandy Hook Elementary shooting, Andy Stanley, pastor of North Point Community Church in Alpharetta, Georgia, noted that many of us have created God in our own images. He explained that there is a God we "put in our back pocket, that we carry around in case of emergencies," the "come to my rescue God," or the "God that doesn't allow bad things to happen to good people."

"I don't believe that God exists," says Stanley. "... from the Old Testament to the New Testament, God is in the midst of pain, leverages pain and, here's the key, redeems pain for good because God is a redeemer."[5]

If you're asking, "Where was God when (fill in the blank) happened?" you need to know this *truth*: God was in the same place as when His Son was hanging on the cross for your sins and for mine . . . and when Jesus said, "My God, my God, why have You forsaken me?" Philip Yancey explains it this way: "The cross demolishes for all time the basic assumption that life will be fair."[6]

Lisa points out this passage from Isaiah 46:5-11 that brought fresh insight to her seething heart.

> To whom will you compare me or count me equal? To whom will you liken me that we may be compared? Some pour out gold from their bags and weigh out silver on the scales; they hire a goldsmith to make it into a god, and they bow down and worship it. They lift it to their shoulders and carry it; they set it up in its place, and there it stands. From that spot it cannot move. Though one cries out to it, it does not answer; it cannot save him from his troubles. Remember this, fix it in mind, take it to heart, you rebels. Remember the former things, those of long ago; I am God, and there is no other; I am God, and there is none like me. I make known the end from the beginning, from ancient times, what is still to come. I say: My purpose will stand, and I will do all that I please. From the east I sum-

mon a bird of prey; from a far-off land, a man to fulfill my purpose. What I have said, that will I bring about, what I have planned, that will I do.

Lisa's skewed image of the true God had left her disappointed, angry and in a terrible state. In His love, God tore away that image and replaced it with a true picture of Himself...one that never leaves us shattered, but instead makes us whole. "My biggest problem was not the death of my son. My biggest problem was a need to release my grudge to God. I'm not saying it was easy. There are many layers to releasing a grudge." But amazingly, and as simple as it sounds, Lisa woke up one morning and the anger was gone. What was left was restoration with God and, therefore, others.

God has used this wonderfully awful/awfully wonderful experience to plant in Lisa a deep desire to see women transformed through the power of God's Word. She was always a gifted communicator, but her "Untestimony" shines brighter than any perfect story ever could, making her a go-to woman for others experiencing devastating loss. Lisa had planned on a life with a testimony that showed God's goodness because of her faithfulness. But instead, her "Untestimony" displays God's goodness because of *His* faithfulness.

No one likes to admit they're angry. We can admit we're disappointed, confused, or caught off guard. But mad? Well, it just doesn't make us look very good.

The moment I found my father, I experienced a quick flash of anger.

The loss of my father, the knowledge that he chose to leave this world, and the knowledge that of all the wonderful conversations we had had through the years he would let the one we had a few days earlier be the last one between us...was truly more than I could bear. For a brief moment I was angry with him. Then compassion overshadowed anger, as I considered the excruciating feelings he must have experienced to believe that suicide was the best alternative. For several months, my main focus was on the emotional pain my father must have experienced those last hours.

Five months later, I awakened from that stupor to realize I was outraged. Outraged with my father for not sticking around for his grandsons and instead leaving them with a legacy of quitting. Furious that he exited without making some things right with Mark that he should've made right. Offended that he left, not giving us a chance to talk out what happened on that terrible Thursday. Angry that for the rest of my life, that would be my last conversation with a father whom I loved deeply.

My anger spilled over to God. Alcohol-free for the first time in decades, my dad had been doing so well. "This was not the end of the story I had in mind, God!"

God already knows your pain, your anger, and your inability to handle it. But you need to get it off your chest and give it to God.

There is so much to this life that doesn't make sense. Any quick, pretty answer about suffering falls flat, sounding like hot air and feeling like plastic. When Job demanded an explanation for all his troubles, God told him, "You wouldn't understand."

As time passes, the painful words and their consequences visit me less and less often. But occasionally something happens and there's an unexpected sting. To be honest, as I typed these words today, I shed a few tears remembering that Thursday. I'd chop a body part off not to have had that conversation. But since it did happen and I can't change it, it's become an opportunity to go to the cross with it every time it comes up.

God already knows your pain, your anger, and your inability to handle it. But you need to get it off your chest and give it to God. What would getting it off your chest look like? Maybe it involves driving alone down a country road where nobody's going to hear you shout, cry and pound your steering wheel. Then drive away from that place, leaving your words behind. Maybe it's writing a note to God, then burning it. Or writing on a helium balloon, then releasing it into the sky.

I admit these things sound a little childlike, but they allow you to tangibly release the thing that's tearing you apart. Do it your way. But the point is to get somewhere where you can be gut-level honest with God and confide in Him the deepest, darkest despair of your heart.

What are some of the things you might say to God?

"I can't take this pain one more day."
"God, I'm losing my mind. I don't think I'm going to come through this in one piece."
"God, with friends like You, who needs enemies?"
"God, what on earth were you THINKING?"

Or perhaps something like this entry I penned in my journal during a hard time in my twenties, "God, either you don't see me, or you don't care. And I think you see me just fine."

Being honest with God can be messy. But, surprisingly, there's freedom in realizing you can't bring back your wandering spouse, heal your little girl, turn your investment around or restore your aging mom's memory. It's at this point we finally find relief in admitting that we are not God. This is where healing begins...when we admit to God, and to ourselves, that our trial is truly more than we can handle. We cannot fix the unfixable.

So when you're ready to admit it, you're in a great spot. Because now you're ready for the next step.

Take Time to Reflect:

1. If you're in a tough situation right now, at what stage do you see yourself? Are you:
- Confident in your own abilities and resources?
- Trying bravely to put on a happy face and keep up a good front while secretly feeling overwhelmed?
- Striving in vain to control all the circumstances around you?
- Or are you discouraged and in despair, overwhelmed by the trials that surround you?

2. If it's true that God gave some of His choice servants more than they could handle, what encouragement does that bring to you as you face difficult circumstances?

3. Is there some grudge you've been holding toward God? What happens inside you as you reflect on the fact that God holds absolutely no grudge toward you?

CHAPTER SIX

L — Let Go

*"Cast your cares on the Lord and He will sustain you;
He will never let the righteous fall."*

- Psalm 55:22

good book sounded fascinating right about now.

Any book would do.

I just wanted to be anywhere but where I was—about to jump out of a plane. However, my instructor was determined, and I was fastened to him. I let go and the next thing I knew I was hurtling through space at 120 mph!

My friend David Duncan tells the story of having his second leg amputated. Due to diabetes complications, the first had been removed years earlier. Then the fevers came and the second leg burned hot with infection. In addition to David's own prayers, a tidal wave of petitions from friends and loved ones continually flooded the throne room of The Great Physician.

There was much more David wanted to do for the Kingdom. But in his thinking, to be completely without legs and stuck in a wheelchair would make him an invalid…of little use to God or others. He was a children's minister and thought children would be afraid of him. "I thought if I could just keep one leg, I'd be okay. I'd have some semblance of independence and usefulness," he told me, looking back on the ordeal. "But to lose both legs? It was unthinkable."

The infection would subside for a few weeks, then rage again. For seven years, he held on to his second leg. Then sitting in a fast food drive-through line one day, David came to a place of surrender…a place of letting go. "In that line, there was nothing to do but wait," he explains. "I was exhausted from recurring fevers caused by the infected leg." The encounter with God he had was undeniable. He heard God ask, "Why are you holding on to a seven-year anchor?" Suddenly he wasn't afraid. Immediately he made the phone call to set up the surgery.

So how about you? What do you need to let go of?

Let go of your bargaining.

If your storm has lingered, chances are you, too, have done all the things David did: fasted, prayed, stood on the Word, and confessed every sin you can remember—all the way back to junior high! As David jokes, he even confessed his wife Shirley's sins! But perhaps, as in David's case, your storm has continued and God, in His sovereignty, hasn't chosen to remedy the situation.

Friend, it's time to let go of your bargaining with God.

In 1969, Kubler-Ross introduced the five stages of grief and loss: denial, anger, bargaining, depression and, finally, acceptance. She noted that the emotions can occur in any order. (For more information on the five stages of grief, read her book *On Death and Dying*.)

Bargaining seems to be a major part of the grieving process. We don't mind God being God as long as He's God on our terms. As long as His plans fit in with our plans. When we're hurting, we desperately want to strike a deal with God.

What does letting go of bargaining look like? For my friend David, there was a personal history of God's faithfulness. "He had proven true in the past. I didn't need to try to figure anything out or come up with a formula. I didn't want to boss Him. So I finally resigned from being the Master of my universe."

Releasing control might sound something like this (forgive the unorthodox tone...honesty can be messy):

You think You know everything, God? Then here! Here's my problem! YOU take it. (But Lord, I have a few suggestions for how You might want to pro-

ceed from here.) Oh...there I go again. Really. It's Yours. Take it.

Or you may say something like:

God, I've done everything I know to do. I'm worn out from bargaining. For the record, I'm crying 'Uncle'! Please enter my chaos/broken dream/devastated heart, etc. Step onto my Titanic. In other words, take control and do what You see as best.

Or it may simply sound like this:

Help, God. Help.

We cannot bargain with God. We must trust Him.

Let go of your anger toward God.

In the previous chapter I mentioned the importance of admitting our anger to God. It's healthy to tell God the very depths of our anger. And it's not like we're telling God something He doesn't already know. But over time, we must take the next step—to let go of that anger.

What's at the core of what makes us angry? The circumstances may be any number of things. But when it gets right down to it, someone (God or another human being) either did something we don't like or did not do something we thought they should've done. All our bargaining hasn't gotten us the results we wanted. And when we realize our bargaining isn't working, we're tempted to be angry.

Are you angry because you didn't get the results you prayed for? Are you angry because you've surrendered to God, expecting Him to do what you asked Him to do—and He didn't? Have you expected God to keep *His* part of *your* bargain? If so, welcome to the club. I've certainly been there and I've got a hunch you and I aren't the only ones.

You must leave room for God to be God.

But I have to be honest with you. When you choose to surrender to God, I can't tell you that everything is going to turn out just the way you want. Yes, there are wonderful promises you can claim from God's Word. But when we make bargains with God, expecting Him to do exactly what we want Him to do, we're putting ourselves in a very dangerous position.

You must leave room for God to be God. His ways are not our ways. (Isaiah 55:8-9). There are eternal kingdom purposes that we cannot begin to understand. So ask yourself this question: "Am I going to yield to God, participate with His purposes and trust Him with the outcome? Even if it's not the path I would choose?"

How do we begin to let go of our anger toward God? To put it in terms of a human relationship, let me tell you a story that happened to someone I know.

A woman excitedly plans a special surprise weekend for her husband's upcoming birthday. So as not to tip him off, she plans it a few weeks earlier than his actual birthday. Reservations are made at an extravagant hotel out of town. Relatives and close friends are invited.

Two weeks before the special weekend, the husband announces he's attending a seminar on the very weekend of the party and asks her to go with him.

"Is there no other weekend that you can catch the seminar?" she asks.

"No, this is the only weekend it's offered," he replies.

"Um, I may have something that weekend," she stalls while her mind races at the thought of all the details she would need to reschedule.

Angrily, the husband replies, "I can't believe you won't go with me. There's nothing on your calendar...I checked. You just don't want to go."

The wife can settle the dilemma on the spot by explaining everything, but the surprise she's worked so hard to pull off will be spoiled.

Instead, she changes the date for the party, informs the guests, and the guests rearrange their calendars to accommodate the new date. The husband's secretary clears his calendar for the new date. All the while, the husband's angry accusations continue.

"If you really loved me, you would've agreed to go with me immediately. But you hesitated."

Weeks pass with a pouting, angry husband.

On the day of the party, she says to her still pouting husband, "Let's take a trip." She has packed his bags, thinking through every detail of what will be needed for the weekend.

Confused, he agrees. When they walk into the swanky restaurant, family and friends greet him at the long, beautifully decorated table.

"SURPRISE! HAPPY BIRTHDAY!" He enjoys hugs, laughter and well wishes from friends and family he hasn't seen in years. It is a birthday bash for the records.

Later, in the quiet of the evening, he asks his wife, "How did all this happen?"

"Do you remember the weekend of the seminar? That was the original date of the birthday bash I was planning for you. I hesitated because I had so many details to work out in order to change it so you could attend your seminar AND still have a surprise party."

In that moment, the grudge and resentment of the past weeks dissipate like a helium balloon with a hole in it. Indignation melts into indebtedness at the recognition of the loving details planned in his behalf behind the scenes, all while he had fumed. The husband had wrongly interpreted his wife's actions as cruel and uncaring, when in reality a wonderful party was being planned on his behalf.

God is working behind the scenes for an incredible surprise party for you. You may not see the result in this life. But it is coming.

When devastating loss happens to us, it's tempting to interpret God's actions or seeming inaction as being cruel. He could have kept the event from happening, but He didn't. While sorrow and grief are natural responses to loss, anger comes from believing that God does not have our best interest at heart. When struggling with anger, it is helpful to remember that the Bible is full of assurance that God indeed does all things right and that He loves us.

God is working behind the scenes for an incredible surprise party for you. You may not see the result in this life. But it is coming.

I find great comfort from the words of the 18th century poet and hymn writer William Cowper.

> *Judge not the Lord by feeble sense,*
> *But trust Him for His grace;*
> *Behind a frowning providence*
> *He hides a smiling face.*[7]

Don't make the mistake of the husband who angrily accused the very person who was planning an elaborate celebration just for him. You'll end up saying with Job, "Surely I spoke of things I did not understand, things too wonderful for me to know (Job 42:3)."

In the previous chapter, we learned to confess our anger. Now ask God to help you release it to Him.

Let go of your doubt.

In the middle of your storm, all kinds of doubts can assault your mind. One of the most common is the thought, "Is God really on my side?" You may wonder, "Is God getting back at me for some past sin?" No. As Robert Kelleman so beautifully puts it, "God is not getting back at you. Instead, God is getting you back to *Himself.*"[8]

Okay. Yes, God hates sin. He hates it so much that He put all of your sin and mine on Jesus and then punished Him. The full extent of God's wrath was extinguished on His Son. Just before Jesus died, He said,

"It is finished." Finished with what? God was finished dealing with the sin of those who fully trust in His Son's work on the cross. "For I will forgive their wickedness and will remember their sins no more" (Hebrews 8:12).

You may doubt that He has forgiven you because you don't *feel* forgiven. But God calls you and me to believe what *He* says about your confessed sin instead of what *you* say about it.

"Blessed is the man whose sin the Lord does not count against him" (Psalm 32:2).

"As far as the east is from the west, so far has he removed our transgressions from us"(Psalm 103:12).

"If You, O Lord, kept a record of sins, O Lord, who could stand? But with You there is forgiveness; therefore You are feared" (Psalm 130:3-4).

"Therefore, there is now no condemnation for those who are in Christ Jesus" (Romans 8:1).

I know I sound like a cheerleader who's had too much

You may doubt that He has forgiven you because you don't FEEL forgiven. But God calls you and me to believe what HE says about your confessed sin instead of what YOU say about it.

coffee, but I love these verses! And I bet you will, too, if you've ever doubted God's loving forgiveness.

When the accuser reminds you of past sins and failures, remind him that:

"Jesus paid it all,
all to Him I owe,
sin had left a crimson stain,
He washed it white as snow!"[9]

In your storm, His purpose is to cause you to focus and rely on Him. His purpose is to build your confidence and trust in the One who *can* calm your storm.

It takes faith to let go of doubt. And faith is believing God can do His job. Which leads to our next section.

Let go and let God do His job.

Letting God do His job involves a shift in thinking from "I've got this" to "God, please take this." However you express it is up to you. But when that moment comes, a tiny light begins to dawn. And we begin to see that when we think we can fix our problem, when we pretend to be "fine" or

In your storm, His purpose is to cause you to focus and rely on Him. His purpose is to build your confidence and trust in the One who CAN calm your storm.

"brave" in the midst of devastating heartache, we're actually messing it all up. And we may begin to realize that being the "Master of our universe," as my friend David described it, has left us exhausted and secretly cynical while we keep laboring to keep the "Good Christian" act going.

As you relinquish to God your sweaty death grip on your circumstances, something beautiful begins to happen. You are freed from the burden of trying to be God! You realize that God is doing something in your storm…something you may not fully understand. And you begin to sense that He's at work for a good purpose in your life—and in the lives of others. It may not be the way you wanted your prayer answered, but there's real comfort when you remember that His great love for you was settled on the cross. And because of that great love, He's working for His glory and your ultimate good.

It was a Wednesday night at choir rehearsal. Hearts were heavy with the knowledge that David had lost his second leg that morning. As the choir director, I asked, "Has anyone spoken with David today?" A hand went up. "How is he?" I'll never forget the sagging shoulders, the downcast expressions as I scanned the room. Everyone there loved David. The choir member replied, "He's busy deciding how tall he wants to be."

A gasp...then a collective hilarious belly laugh from everyone in the choir.

With a quick wit and lighthearted way, David lights up a room. Each morning, as you and I choose which outfit we're going to wear, David chooses from his repertoire of legs! When he speaks to children and students he sports anything from Camo, Thomas the Train, smiley faces, Sponge Bob Square Pants to Scooby-Doo!

He's been known to pull a prank or two, rigging a leg to "fall off" in deathly serious waiting rooms. His humor and lovable ways disarm perfect strangers, breaking down walls between the disabled and those who aren't. All ages, from children to senior adults, get the message without him ever saying a word. You can see it on their faces.

As David tickles the funny bone, speaks of the wonder of life and points out the goodness of God in his winsome way, people walk away with this thought: "If someone with no legs and a host of other health issues can find hilarious joy in this life, maybe joy is possible for me, too. Maybe I have more to be thankful for than I realized."

David explains, "I've acquired a heart that is sensitive, approachable and caring. I now know how to laugh and cry with others. God's given me the gift of joy."

When David relinquished control, he lost his leg. But he gained a ministry that reaches all kinds of people in all types of situations.

Take Time to Reflect:

1. In what ways have you tried to "make a deal" with God?

2. Have you ever yielded to God, while simultaneously expecting things to turn out your way?

3. In losing his legs, David gained a ministry of joy and comfort for others. What are you holding on to that God may want to exchange for something bigger?

4. Is there some situation that has you angry with God? The Bible assures us that He does all things right and that He loves us deeply. As you let that truth sink in, how does it affect your feelings toward God?

CHAPTER SEVEN

L — Look

"Turn your eyes upon Jesus,
Look full in His wonderful face,
And the things of earth will grow strangely dim
In the light of His glory and grace."[10]

*A*ny last minute words of instruction?" I asked my guide, rather tensely. I wanted to know about pushing away from the airplane, when to pull the ripcord, and he *still* hadn't said anything about how to land. I wanted, no, *I needed* more technical information. His reply? "Yes. Keep your eyes open and enjoy the view." *Oh, what a cut-up. He is getting on my last nerve. This is a life and death matter and he's telling me to enjoy the view! I'm going to talk with his supervisor. That is, if I live.*

A few minutes later, just when I thought my ears would explode, my cheeks flap off my face and my heart thump out of my chest, my guide pulled the ripcord. The deafening roar of air past my ears suddenly vanished, plummeting gave way to floating, and I was engulfed in silence, peace, and a stunning, breathtaking panoramic view of serene countryside. "OH, IT'S SO BEAUTIFUL!" I exclaimed. "Yes," he agreed quietly, "it is." A few minutes earlier I was convinced that my guide's sole purpose was to torture me. But now I heard myself sincerely thanking the same person I'd resisted just moments before. The view was worth the jump. Grumbling became gratitude, protesting became praise.

When we keep our eyes open and LOOK expectantly for His glory, we find much to be thankful for.

Instead of putting on the brakes, my friend Susan (not her real name), then 17, bore down on the car's accelerator as she approached the red light at the busy intersection. Moments before, her locked bedroom door had been violently broken down while she escaped into the cold night through her bathroom window—with nothing but her purse and the clothes on her back. "I was aware at some level of the danger of running the red light. But in that moment, the thought of being caught and killed by my father was far worse than the possibility of colliding with an oncoming car."

The sexual abuse had begun at the age of nine. Sometime later, when Susan told her mother, her mother became severely depressed and twice attempted suicide. The night Susan escaped, she had overheard her father beating her mother in their bedroom. When Susan intervened, her father's wrath turned from her mother to Susan. Susan remembers hearing her mother shouting, "Run, Susan!"

Later, while staying at a friend's home, she met and married a wealthy man. But his money was not the answer to her problems. Her new husband soon fell back into a previous drug habit, began dealing and also introduced Susan to the world of drugs. Twice she was rushed to the emergency room and almost died of cocaine overdose.

During this same time, her grandfather, whom she loved deeply, died. And Susan began to think about eternity. God used the overdose and her grandfather's death to give her a distaste for drugs. She moved out. Then her husband divorced her, because she was "no fun anymore."

While moving her belongings into her tiny, new apartment, she opened a drawer and found a magazine her grandmother had left there. Susan opened the magazine and saw a poem entitled "Surrender." "I knew my heart wanted to surrender everything to Him," she said. She dropped to knees and gave herself to God—troubles and all.

Moments later, someone knocked on her door and invited her to a conference. At the conference, Susan heard about the love of God for the brokenhearted. This was the beginning of her new life.

At the risk of sounding "Cinderella-ish," she soon met a man who loved God and Susan with all his heart. Then, with God's help, she forgave her father. Today Susan is a biblical counselor who is making a difference in the lives of women struggling with a variety of issues. The joy is evident in Susan's life. In fact, I knew

Susan for a few years before I heard her story. When I first learned of her past, I asked incredulously, "How is it that you are so strong, so joyful despite what you've been through?"

With a twinkle in her eye and an infectious laugh, she said, "Because God was with me! He preserved my life when I was crawling out the bathroom window that night. He didn't let me die from a drug overdose. I had a praying grandmother. He brought new friends to my door who introduced me to God. Eventually He brought a loving man into my life."

"God is using my past to help me give insight and encouragement to other women. He was with me then... He is with me now...He will be with me in whatever comes!" Her daily prayer is to "rest in His sovereignty and rely on His grace," remembering that "the same grace that was there for me in the past will most certainly be available and sufficient in the future."

In the middle of her circumstances, Susan looked for reasons to be thankful, saw God in every detail and now looks for people to comfort.

Look for reasons to be thankful.

The fact that I'm not God and you're not God is enough to be thankful for. But there's more to say grace over than just that.

Thank Him for any little goodness you see in your situation. If you can't think of anything, thank Him that you're still here. Maybe you don't *want* to be here, but if you are still here, there is a reason. And the reason is: He's not finished with you. There is still more He wants to do in you and through you. There is still purpose for your life.

When a child of God looks up from the ash heap of what used to be his life and praises God, the powers of darkness tremble. That kind of praise, in the midst of terrible circumstances, is almost too much to comprehend. But it opens the door for God to use that situation to touch multiple lives...and that terrifies the enemy.

When a child of God looks up from the ash heap of what used to be his life and praises God, the powers of darkness tremble.

Look for God in every detail.

When I was in the depths of my grief, I discovered that the weight of my heavy heart started to lift whenever I focused on 'seeing' God's glory and adoring Him.

C.S. Lewis said, "Gratitude exclaims, very properly, 'How good of God to give me this.' Adoration says, 'What must be the quality of that Being whose far-off and momentary coruscations [flashes of light] are like this?' One's mind runs back up the sunbeam to the sun."[11]

When we spend time reflecting on the attributes of the Giver, our minds run "back up the sunbeam to the sun." Our focus shifts from our pain to the generosity of God. That is when joy begins to seep back into our devastated hearts.

God is always with us. He promises He will never leave us or forsake us (Joshua 1:5, Genesis 28:15). Yet, there are rare and precious moments when we experience His presence in a more tangible way. We have all known people who tell us that a particular experience was "the hardest thing I've ever gone through." Then they add, "But I felt the presence of God in the most remarkable way."

Look for ways He makes His presence known to you in your journey of grief. Here are a few examples:

- A scripture that you've read many times suddenly springs to life with new meaning.
- The kindness of a friend.
- Interesting circumstances you know were meant just for you that bring comfort.
- Gratitude for simple moments of joy that perhaps you didn't recognize before.
- The new compassion you feel for others who grieve.

- Finding yourself reaching out to others during their time of grief.
- The platform you now have to bring comfort to others.

The flood of love that came to us during our devastating loss was overwhelming. We felt the love of Christ in every tender act, listening ear, and word of comfort.

Psalm 107:19-20 encourages us that God meets us in our distress and heals us with His Word. There are two particular instances that stand out to me when God specifically met me in my distress.

I'm a little embarrassed to confess this, but during the first three weeks after my dad died, I would call his cell phone, just to hear his voice. "Hi, this is Bill," the recording said. "I'm not available at the moment, but if you'll leave your name and number, I'll gladly get back with you just as soon as I can." Hearing him say that he 'wasn't available at the moment' somehow eased the chronic lump in my throat during those first few weeks. It reminded me that I would see him again one day, just not right now.

I didn't tell anyone I was calling his number because I felt so ridiculous. One day I called the number and, unexpectedly, a robotic, recorded voice informed me that the number was no longer in service. Alarmed, I told John that Dad's number had been disconnected. Having no idea that I called the number several times a day, he replied, "Yes, I had it disconnected." I disintegrated into tears. Almost frantically I admitted, "I call his number to hear his voice and now it's gone." Even more childishly I asked, "Is there a way to call the phone company and get it back?" John said, "Oh, Honey, I didn't know. I didn't see any reason to keep the account." Sounding like a five-year-old, I said, "I just wasn't ready for his voice to go away."

But here's our precious God.

That same week, a man called and introduced himself as the manager of a local radio station. Long ago my father had been nicknamed "the man with the golden voice." Through the years he had done work as a radio announcer and had also done voice-overs for commercials. The manager said, "Connie, you don't know me, but I knew your father. I have in my archives several recordings of commercials he did for us. This is a long shot, but I was wondering if those recordings might be something you'd be interested in having?" "Yes!" I exclaimed.

God is so good. He even used the kindness of this stranger to minister to me in my healing process.

The road of grief is never a smooth, uphill climb. It's jagged and messy. You think you're doing well, and then there's an unexpected day of tears. But God meets us in our distress…like He did in this second instance.

A year after my dad's death, I needed his Social Security Number for some documentation. Where in the world could I find that? Then it occurred to me that it would be on his death certificate. So on my lunch hour, I drove home to get that errand out of the way. In my car was a CD that I had been meaning to preview for the choir I directed. It had been on the front seat of my car for several days. When I pulled into my driveway, I put the CD into the player so I could listen to it on the way back to work.

In the closet, I pulled down the box where my dad's things were stored: pictures, letters, odds and ends, and his death certificate. What happened next was so unexpected. I just needed his Social Security Number. But words leaped off the document in a fresh and shocking way. CAUSE OF DEATH: SELF-INFLICTED GUNSHOT WOUND. A surprising wave of grief enveloped me.

The awful sorrow, regret and "if onlys" came rushing back over me. I had been doing so well! But now I sank to my knees and prayed through hot tears, "I cannot bear this grief anymore, God. It's too heavy. Please carry it for me."

I dried my eyes, sighed, wrote down the needed information and, with a heavy heart, got in the car to return to work.

As I cranked the car, the CD began to play. A narrator spoke these words: *He was despised and re-*

jected of men; a man of sorrows, and acquainted with grief: and we hid as it were our faces from him; he was despised, and we esteemed him not. Surely he hath borne our griefs, and carried our sorrows: yet we did esteem him stricken, smitten of God, and af-flicted (Isaiah 53:3-4 KJV).

I had prayed those very words just moments before: "I can't bear this grief. It's too heavy. Please carry it for me."

And His response? "Surely He has borne our griefs, and carried our sorrows."

In that moment I was reminded that God was with me, "acquainted with my sorrows," was here to bear my griefs and would see me through this valley. I was ener-gized, strengthened and renewed by His unmistakable presence. Heaviness of heart turned to honest praise.

My greatest praise in the midst of my storm was for my father's salvation. Since the age of nine when I came to know the Lord, I had carried concern for my father. Through the years, we had conversations about spiri-tual matters and each time I came away from those conversations with a sense that my dad did not know the Lord. I fretted. I prayed. I fretted some more.

But as I mentioned earlier, during the five months he lived with me, I came to know that my father had indeed trusted in the Lord for salvation. It was a mustard seed of faith, but it was undeniable. I will forever be grateful that, because of God's mercy and grace, I will see my father again. And I'm also grateful that God made sure I knew that I would!

Be on the lookout for God in every detail of your life. He's there—working for your good.

Look for people to comfort.

You won't need to look very hard or very far. When people know what you've been through, God will use your journey to build a platform that will glorify Him and comfort others.

Be on the lookout for God in every detail of your life. He's there—working for your good.

When a suicide happens in my community, I often get a phone call. These calls come from friends and strangers. Before my experience, I didn't know what to say or do when I received the news that a friend had lost a loved one. Now I know.

I know that I don't have to have anything wise or wonderful to say. And neither do you. All we need to do is show up.

God has golden nuggets of truth to share with you in your trial. He's not going to leave you here. He's going to bring you through it, or He's going to give you the grace to endure it. Either way, He's giving you a testimony and He's going to use you to encourage and minister to other folks for years to come in ways that you cannot even imagine at this moment. In our deepest sorrows, God will show us His brightest glory. We must not, as Job's wife suggested, "curse God and die." Instead we must humbly submit to our sovereign God who does all things well. We must ask Him to show us His glory.

Take Time to Reflect:

1. What are some of the hidden benefits in your life's unwanted situation?

2. When have you felt the kindness of a friend in your situation?

3. Who can you reach out to who's experiencing a hard time?

4. God's promise in Psalm 107:19-20 is that He comes to us in our distress and He heals us with His Word. Can you think of specific ways in which God has met you in your distress? How has God's Word impacted you in your journey of "falling up?"

CHAPTER EIGHT

Living With A Limp

*"The sun rose above him [Jacob] . . .
and he was limping because of his hip."*

- Genesis 32:31

*"Beware of any Christian leader
who does not walk with a limp."*

- A.W. Tozer

After several months have passed, some people will tell you to "get over it." Or that it's "time to move on." These are well-meaning friends—but they haven't walked where you have walked.

You may feel you'll never be the same again. I know that's true for me. The event of my father's suicide stands as a monumental marker on the timeline of my life. Everything—and I mean everything—falls into the category of either "before my dad committed suicide" or "after my dad committed suicide." The clothes I own. The songs I know. The people I've met. The places I've been. Eating a food my father enjoyed. Seeing a movie and thinking, "My dad would go bonkers over that!"

The most random things remind me of the gaping hole left in my heart by my father's choice. He was my greatest encourager. Even now, after several years have passed, whenever I receive exciting news, my reaction in the first nanosecond is to think how elated my dad will be when he hears it. In the next nanosecond, I remember he's not here.

No. I will never be the same.

However, I have learned that I am not alone. Others who have walked a similar path through devastating loss have been graciously transparent to share that, as much as they love God and as much as they desire to see Him glorified in their experience, they, too, are not the same. Like Jacob, they walk with a limp.

Joni Eareckson Tada

A diving accident left her a quadriplegic at age 17, too paralyzed to act on the resulting suicidal urges. But she found faith in God that caused her to do much more than just survive. Now a best-selling author and artist and founder and president of Joni and Friends, she creates beautiful pictures by holding a paintbrush in her teeth. Her life and ministry have impacted millions over the past few decades.

But listen to her gut level honesty:

"I thought, 'This is it. My life is over.'" She prayed one night, "God, if I can't die, please show me how to live. I don't like paralysis; I'm not prepared for this. This is not what I bargained for."

"The weaker I became, the harder I had to lean on Him. But the harder I leaned on Him, the stronger I discovered Him to be."

"Don't be thinking I'm spiritually strong. I'm no veteran at this paralysis thing. I'm not a professional quadriplegic. I wake up in the morning many times, and I'll hear my girlfriend come in the front door. And she'll be running water for coffee in the kitchen, and I know she's going to come in my bedroom in a minute. And she's going to give me a bed bath, get me dressed, sit me in a wheelchair, brush my hair, brush my teeth, blow my nose.

"And there are times I'm still having my eyes closed thinking, God, I have no strength for this. I can't face this. I can't—I have no resources for this. I have no smile for this woman.

"But you do, God. You have strength. You have resources. Can I please borrow your smile? And by the time my girlfriend comes through the door with that cup of coffee and a happy good morning, I can give her a smile already hard fought for, already won straight from heaven."[12]

Tony Dungy

Tony Dungy, former head coach of the Indianapolis Colts, is a well-respected hero on and off the field. He's a role model for many throughout the NFL, for families and for those touched by his ministry work. His genuineness regarding his son's suicide encourages those who have experienced loss. He shares, "Lauren and

I knew our only option was to trust God and let Him lead us through the pain...our job was to persevere and follow the Lord no matter what."[13]

In addition, his words spoken at the 19th Annual Athletes in Action Super Bowl Breakfast in 2006 touch me deeply, because this man does not pretend to be completely over it. "I'm not totally recovered, I don't know if I ever will be, it's still ever-painful," he said, wiping back a tear. "But some good things have come out of it."[14]

Kay Warren

Rick and Kay Warren, co-founders of Saddleback Church in Lake Forest, California, co-hosted the groundbreaking event "The Gathering of Mental Health and the Church" on March 28, 2014. In this historic, first-time gathering of leaders from both the evangelical and Catholic communities, there were discussions on the importance of churches working together to address critical mental health issues.

"We do this in honor and memory of our son and others lost to mental illness, realizing there is hope for others dealing with this condition,"[15] Kay Warren told reporters.

God is using the loss of their son to suicide for great blessing in this fallen world. But listen to Kay's straight talk when it comes to the subject of "getting over it" and "moving on."

> They want the old Rick and Kay back. They secretly wonder when things will get back to normal for us – when we'll be ourselves, when the tragedy of April 5, 2013 will cease to be the grid that we pass everything across. And I have to tell you – the old Rick and Kay are gone. They're never coming back. We will never be the same again.[16]

Yes, like Jacob, these people walk with a limp. But it is a holy limp.

Genesis 32:22-32 records the story of Jacob, who had an experience with an angel of God that changed his life forever. In the process of wrestling with the angel, his thigh was touched, resulting in his walking with a limp for the rest of his days, demonstrating his dependence on the Lord. In other words, his physical strength was reduced to weakness. Yet the impact of that night's battle was such that God changed his name from Jacob (meaning "trickster") to Israel (meaning "he struggles with God" or "ruling with God"). In spite of his new weakness—in fact, *because* of his new weakness—God gave him a new name and a position of authority.

Rodney Francis, Director of *The Gospel Faith Messenger*, writes, "When God marks us – and leaves us with a limp – we discover more spiritual authority than we've ever known before. The enemy is not afraid of a limp, but of the power that that God-ordained limp represents."[17]

I believe Jacob's limp represented a new dependence on God.

Jennifer Rothschild

Internationally known speaker Jennifer Rothschild, author of nine books and founder of Fresh Grounded Faith events and womensministry.net, became blind at age fifteen and now helps others walk by faith, not by sight. Jennifer knows God can heal her blindness. But to date, for reasons known only to Him, He has not chosen to do so. In her book, *God is Just Not Fair*, she speaks of her own wrestling match with God.

> Like Jacob, I have also clung to God in the darkness of my blindness and in the darkness of my confusion and disappointment. God has injured me to bless me, and now that very injury is part of the blessing. He has taught me as I wrestle with Him not to choose flight but to choose a holy fight – an unwillingness to let go of God until he uses this injury to bless me. Encouraging others to stay in the fight with God, she asks, Could your injury be God's perfect way of blessing you – his perfectly strange way?[18]

Three Responses to Suffering

None of the people I've mentioned, whether ancient or modern day, pretend to be the same as before. They have all been changed. You cannot go through losses like they've gone through and remain the same.

And I've noticed that people tend to have one of three responses when heartbreak hits.

1. Ignore and Stuff
   One response is to stuff the painful event far away, as if you put it on the back shelf of the closet of your heart, hoping the painful emotions will just go away. But they won't. This occurs a lot with a shaming event such as sexual abuse. It feels too awful, too terrible to talk about, so we just lock it inside. But the unaddressed event carries power. The heartbreak becomes lodged in our hearts and, as a result, we ourselves become "stuck." Stuck in our woundedness, our lack of trust, our belief that "life is hard, and then you die." That wound needs lancing. The way to release the poison is in telling your story—not to just anyone, but to a trusted friend. Alcoholics Anonymous has a saying: "You're as sick as your secrets." It seems illogical, but when we share our story, the hold on us it's had all these years begins to weaken. There is a cleansing that comes from confession to a trusted friend.

2. Tell Anyone and Everyone

   Another response is to repeatedly shout our story from the rooftops to anyone and everyone that will listen. Not with the purpose of cleansing our hearts, but rather to declare over and over (and over again) how we've been "done wrong," either by God or by others. This response keeps a person in victim mode, always the helpless casualty of a particularly painful event. Ten, twenty, thirty years may go by, but the story never changes. And their heart never changes. Frozen in time and inwardly focused, they remain bitter, cynical, seething with hatred, still playing the victim role long after the event is over. When confronted with these destructive attitudes and behaviors, this person is fond of rehearsing his hurts, then concluding with something like, "And that's why I'm the way that I am. End of story."

3. Your Story for His Glory

   And then occasionally you meet someone whose painful event has caused them to surrender, abandoning all hope of solving the problem or healing the pain on their own, becoming ever dependent on God, and always looking expectantly for His glory in their unwanted circumstance. It's not all wrapped up neatly with a pretty bow. They still have unanswered questions. There are tears on occasion. But their painful event now serves, not as a justification for their behavior, but as a testimony to God's grace in their lives. Through the tears, there's a submission to His will resulting in a more tender heart, an outward focus, and a compassion for others who hurt. There is brokenness, yes. But there is also joy. No, they are not "over it." Nor do they ever need to be. Why? Because their story is for His glory.

Joni Eareckson Tada, Tony Dungy, Kay Warren, and Jennifer Rothschild have surrendered their stories to God—and He is using them for His glory. They confess their tears to God and to us. And it is those same tears that give them a platform of credibility and hope for others who are hurting. They don't begin to understand loss. Nor do they pretend to have it all figured out. What I hear in their words—and what I know to be true for me—is this declaration: God, I don't know what You're doing. I don't understand it. I don't like it. But I'm Yours.

"God, I don't know what you're doing. I don't understand it. I don't like it. But I'm Yours."

Today may you begin to walk in freedom—freedom from the false burden of having to be "over it." Yes, you may be broken. Yes, you may walk with a limp. But, like Jacob, you are new.

Declare with us: "God, I don't know what You're doing. I don't understand it. I don't like it. But I'm Yours."

Now walk forward with a holy limp and see God do for you and through you what only He can do.

Take Time to Reflect

1. What have you experienced that has left you walking with a limp?

2. How are you not the same?

3. Are there ways in which you find yourself more dependent on God?

4. Like Joni, have you found God to be your strength in your weakness? If so, how?

5. In what ways do you see God using your unwanted experience, your holy limp, for the good of others and for His glory?

CHAPTER NINE

My Strange Dream Comes True

"For the Lord will go before you,
the God of Israel will be your rear guard."

- Isaiah 52:12

Do you remember the puzzling dream I told you about at the beginning? Remember how I was more joyful than I'd ever been, with my hands extended straight up in the air? But mysteriously I was on the front center row of my church, a place I had never sat before?

One week after the dream, as our friend Mac closed my father's memorial service, he did away with the myth that "to commit suicide was the unpardonable sin." He said, "If Bill had not trusted Jesus Christ, then today would be a sad day…a sad day indeed. Who knows why Bill did what he did? He couldn't measure up and those feelings of inferiority overtook him. Life caved in on him, he wasn't thinking clearly and he made a terrible choice. But before the sound of the shot was even heard, his spirit was at home and Jesus met him with outstretched arms and said, 'Bill! Welcome home!' And for the first time ever, Bill was convinced that he was loved, that he had value and that God had placed on him the same value He had placed on His Son, Jesus. And Bill said, 'I'm valuable. I'm accepted. I'm accepted in the Beloved!'"

And then Mac suggested that my dad began to sing,
"And when before the throne
I stand in Him, complete,
Jesus died my soul to save,
My lips shall e'er repeat.
Jesus paid it all,
All to Him I owe,
Sin had left a sinful stain,
He washed it white as snow."[19]

And then our worship leader began to lead the song
"Grace, grace, God's grace,
grace that is greater than all my sin."[20]

And then into
"When we've been there ten thousand years,
bright shining as the sun,
we've no less days to sing God's praise
than when we've first begun."[21]

It was in that moment of high praise to our God of grace that I realized, for the first time in my life, my hands were in the air. These conservative hands were straight up in praise and adoration that God had given my father what he could never have earned himself—the robes of righteousness! God's Word was true. Nothing—not even the terrible choice of suicide—could separate my father from the love of Christ.

Jesus had indeed paid it all! As I realized my hands were raised, it dawned on me that I was in the same place I had been in my dream the week before: on the floor with the congregation, not on the platform where I was normally found. In the front middle pew, not on the side where I usually sat. And suddenly the puzzling mystery was solved.

It was my father's funeral. In my dream a week earlier, I was sitting where I was now, where family members sit during their loved one's funeral.

As the people sang, I realized my Savior had gone before me, was behind me and would walk with me through this journey of inexplicable sorrow. I don't have to figure it all out. He will hold this mystery until the day I see Him face to face. Hallelujah! I can't wait!

I don't know what your situation is today. But I do know that He is calling you with love and tenderness to trust

Because God wins, we win.

Him with the pieces of the puzzle you can't put together. We don't have to pretend to understand it all. We can face and embrace the mysteries of life because our sovereign, powerful, loving God holds it for us.

Billy Graham once said, "I only know I've read the last page...and God wins." Because God wins, we win. Looking at the tapestries of our lives, we may see only random threads appearing to lead nowhere. Tangled knots. Ugliness. But one day God will flip those tapestries over and we'll see the unbelievable beauty He was weaving into our lives. In that moment, we'll fall to our knees and exclaim, "O, God, you are so good!"

Are you falling today? Remember to F.A.L.L.

F. Focus
　　On finding joy
　　On preaching to yourself
　　On God's truth
A. Admit
　　That it's more than you can handle
　　Your anger to God
L. Let Go
　　Of your bargaining
　　Of your anger toward God
　　Of your doubt
　　And let God do His job
L. Look
　　For reasons to be thankful
　　For God in every detail
　　For people to comfort

F.A.L.L. into His arms and you'll find Him to be every-thing you will ever need.

EPILOGUE

Some would say the enemy had the last word in my father's life. I believe the enemy had the next to the last word. Jesus had the last word.

For the believer, not even the terrible choice of taking one's own life is enough to nullify the grace of God. Nothing can keep us from the love of God (Romans 8:38-39) and no one can snatch you out of His hand (John 10:28).

And for those in whose world the bottom has dropped out and it feels as if you are surely falling, guess what? Happily, this is where our metaphor of "falling" breaks down. You see, the believer may *feel* she

Your faith may seem to be fading out of sight...but not out of God's sight.

is falling, but God will not let her fall. Your faith may seem to be fading out of sight...but not out of God's sight. Your faith is not dependent on your holding onto God, but rather on God holding onto *you*, and He is not about to let go!

When my skydiving instructor fastened himself to me, from that point forward, I was his responsibility. And so it is with God. By the way, when the parachute opened, my guide said calmly, "Now, let's talk about landing. At my cue, straighten your legs, raise your feet and hold that position." This made no sense. I had seen others land (or attempt to land) on their feet and run a little ways. But, as the ground rapidly rose to meet us, he said, "Now." I did as told and was seated gently, like a leaf floating to earth.

During the entire trip, I had worried about landing. Only at the end did I realize he had told me exactly what I needed to know...exactly when I needed to know it. So much of life is spent worrying and crying over: *Is God going to see me through this? Does he hear my prayers? Does He know what I'm going through?* Dear friend, God is with you in your journey. He will see you safely home. Maybe not in the way you think He should. But He does all things well. Occasionally He graciously gives us glimpses of His glorious works. But one day, you'll see the whole story. You'll see behind the scenes of your suffering. And in that moment, you will see everything your gracious God did to get you safely home.

"To him who is able to keep you from falling and to present you before his glorious presence without fault and with great joy – to the only God our Savior be glory, majesty, power and authority, through Jesus Christ our Lord, before all ages, now and forevermore! Amen (Jude 24-25)."

RESOURCES

For Loved Ones of Suicide: Healing Truths to Know and Live By

If you have lost a loved one to suicide, you feel stunned, confused, hurt and betrayed. As you face unanswerable questions, I'd like to share with you truths that helped me and brought me comfort as I wrestled with and grieved my father's suicide. Through this dark experience I found that the promises and presence of God are real. When walking through this painful time, I pray you will find comfort as you soak your mind and heart in the following truths.

1. **We don't know why God allowed this, when it was within His power to stop it.**
   Sometimes God intervenes in a suicide attempt and at other times He doesn't. Although God has all knowledge, there are some things He doesn't tell us.
   "The secret things belong to the Lord our God" (Deuteronomy 29:29).

   "For My thoughts are not your thoughts, neither are your ways my ways, declares the Lord. As the heavens are higher than the earth, so are My ways higher than your ways and my thoughts than your thoughts" (Isaiah 55:8-9).

"Now we see but a poor reflection as in a mirror; then we shall see face to face. Now I know in part; then I shall know fully, even as I am fully known" (1 Corinthians 13:12).

2. **The feeling of massive guilt is common, if not universal, among loved ones of suicide.**
Every conversation and act is revisited over and over. If there is something you feel guilty about, tell the Lord "the whole truth and nothing but the truth" regarding your feelings. Let Him cleanse you. Then know this: the burden of responsibility for this suicide rests solely on the shoulders of the one who chose it. We don't make anyone die by suicide. Do not take on what is not yours to bear.

3. **Suicide is not the unpardonable sin.**
Whatever momentary weakness or feeling of hopelessness caused your loved one to take his life is a mystery. But the final act of suicide is just as forgiven as the final act of murder, theft, gossip or any other sin.

The Bible tells us that our destiny is determined not by our works, but by our trust in the righteousness of Jesus Christ. "For it is by grace you have been saved, through faith – and this not from yourselves, it is the gift of God – not by works, so that no one can boast" (Ephesians 2:8-9).

We sometimes hear the claim that since a person didn't have time to repent of his sins, he must be in hell.

But suppose I have an awful argument with my husband in which I am completely in the wrong, then, in anger and pride, spew vicious words, slam the door on the way out, jump into my car, run a red light, get hit by a truck and die instantly. I did not have time to repent, nor was I in any mood to repent! Would I go to heaven?

The biblical answer is "Yes!" *By faith alone*, Jesus Christ's sacrifice earned for me His righteousness, when I trusted Him as my Lord and Savior. To make the last act of a person's life so supremely important is to misunderstand the incredible grace of our Lord.

If you don't know for sure that your loved one had trusted Christ, entrust him to God. The Bible offers hope even for the person who has been away from God all his life. (I'm not referring to the false hope that all who die regardless of faith will go to heaven. I take Jesus seriously when He says that there is a heaven and a hell, and all of us will someday see one or the other.) Luke records the story of the thief on the cross who called to Jesus for mercy: "Then he said, 'Jesus, remember me when you come into your kingdom.' Jesus answered him, 'I tell you the

truth, today you will be with me in paradise'"
(Luke 23:42-43). Jesus himself says that a heart
change at the last moment is sufficient. Those
who call upon the Lord will be saved.

Who's to say whether or not someone in their
final moments did business with God and
made things right? We must be willing to live
with mystery.

4. **Grieve.**
   Weep until you cannot weep anymore. A few
   months later, when your weeping subsides, you
   may realize that you are very angry. This is good
   and natural and is evidence that you are beginning to come out of your deepest grief. And you
   have a right to be angry. Work out your anger in
   ways that are not hurtful to yourself or others.
   (Punch a pillow, go for a run, swim laps, etc.)

5. **Write a letter to your loved one.**
   One of the most insidious aspects of suicide is
   that there is no closure, no opportunity to say
   goodbye or to resolve conflicts that may have
   contributed to the event. In writing a letter to
   your loved one, say all the things you wanted
   to say but didn't. List any regrets, express your
   outrage toward the person, recount the ways
   that his or her decision affected you and other family members, tell him what you wish he
   had done instead. Write about your feelings

concerning your loved one and the choice he made. Say it all. Then speak of your love for him and things you miss about him. Finally, by God's grace, forgive him. Entrust him to God as you tell him goodbye.

6. **Avoid revisiting the final moment.**
To dwell more on the final moment than the rest of your loved one's life is a dishonor to him. Your cherished memories of tender, proud and hilarious moments are just as important as his final moment. This will require discipline of the mind, especially if you are the one who discovered the body. Having discovered my father's body, I was particularly troubled and haunted by the visual scene. My friend, Dan Darden, a pastoral counselor, shared this very simple, yet helpful technique for dealing with troubling thoughts:

- If you are in a place where you can do this, without people looking at you like you've lost your mind, say out loud, "STOP!" This will jolt the brain and actually interrupt the thought. (I don't recommend it during church or at the movies!) If you are in a public place and cannot say it out loud, then say it very strongly in your mind.

- Be ready with a true, wonderful and comforting thought to replace the former thought. This may be the knowledge that your loved one was a believer in Christ and is out of misery and is fully healed and whole. If you don't know for certain that your loved one was a believer, rejoice in the fact that suicide does not mean that hell is the default destination. Rejoice that God knew your loved one and his circumstances better than you and He is perfect in justice, kindness and mercy. He does all things right.

7. **Don't throw your pictures out.**
In the first weeks and months after my dad died, seeing pictures of him that were scattered around my house caused me deep heartache. When I mentioned this to a friend, her advice was to throw the pictures away, since they were sources of pain. She said getting rid of them might be helpful in moving forward.

Instead of throwing them away, I simply *put* them away. After three or four years, I began to pull a few favorites out. I'm so glad I still have them! I am now able to enjoy, through pictures of my dad, the reminder of happy days in the past as well as those to come.

If you've recently lost a loved one to suicide, avoid the rash decision to throw out your pictures. In simply storing them away, you accomplish two things: 1) you don't have to look at them right now if you don't want to, and 2) you keep the option open of having them later.

8. Eventually, comfort others with the comfort God has given you.

"Praise be to the God and Father of our Lord Jesus Christ, the Father of compassion and the God of all comfort, who comforts us in all our troubles, so that we can comfort those in any trouble with the comfort we ourselves have received from God" (2 Corinthians 1:3-4).

God is going to bring you through this. And He's going to give you incredible truths, forged within your fire. When He does that, bring comfort to others with what He's done for you.

God is going to bring you through this. And He's going to give you incredible truths, forged within your fire. When He does that, bring comfort to others with what He's done for you.

What to Say to a Grieving Heart

When we first get the news that a friend has lost a loved one, it's pretty universal to have feelings of helplessness. After you bring the casserole, then what? What do you say?

You want to express your love, but you don't want to intrude.

Here are a few suggestions:
- Acknowledge the loss.
  Through that first year, the best gifts I received were from the brave souls that dared to ask how I was doing. Most people take the view that the warden did at Folsom Prison, back when Johnny Cash did a concert for the prisoners. The warden cautioned Johnny, "Mr. Cash? Might I suggest you refrain from playing any tunes that remind them, the inmates that is, that they are in prison?"

  Johnny Cash replied, "You think they forgot?" Believe me, when someone loses a loved one, the fact is constantly on her mind. You are not going to "make them sad" by bringing it up. In fact, they will appreciate the fact that you asked how they were doing and that you still remember their loved one.

- Express concern. Say simply, "I am so sorry that happened."

- Be real about your own feelings. "I don't know what to say. I just want you to know I care about you." Statements like this go a long way.

At a party several months after my father's death, a man who was my father's age leaned over to me and said quietly, "I hope I don't bring you pain by mentioning this, and I'm not sure if I should bring it up, but I'd just like to tell you that I thought your father was a remarkable man." What wonderful words those were. How grateful I was for someone who was willing to put his concern for me ahead of his awkward feelings about the subject. I smiled as I assured him, "Your words bring me no pain at all, only comfort and joy. Thanks for telling me."

And speaking of that, let's not require people to respond perfectly to us when they are trying to offer comfort. Be thankful for every gesture of grace, even if it doesn't come off perfectly.

- Offer support.
  Ask simply, "What can I do for you?" This takes it a step further than "if there's anything I can do for you, let me know." Asking what you can do for them communicates that you're more than just a bystander. You want to be involved in your friend's life. If she can't think of anything, make some suggestions. "May I take your kids to school?" "I'm headed to the grocery store. What can I get for you?" Make a couple of meals that she can put in the freezer for later, when all the funeral food is gone.

- Check in with her as time goes by.
The first Thanksgiving, first Christmas, first birthday, etc. are significant. The three-month juncture also seems to be a very important time for people. The funeral is over, the casseroles have all been eaten, the cards have dwindled and others have gone back to life as usual. But your friend is still grieving and will be for several more months, or even the next year. So you're communicating a ton of love when you take the time to say, "How are you doing?"

When people are in grief, they're not looking for someone to take all the pain away. They're just looking for someone to walk with them in the pain.

A few days before the first Father's Day without my dad, I received a card in the mail from a friend. *How kind*, I thought. The next day, I received another half dozen, expressing love for me and gratitude that my father was among the saved. Before the weekend was over, I had received nearly one hundred cards of love and remembrance of my dad on this special weekend. Armed with the love of friends, I faced Father's Day, not as a victim of grief, but as a grateful worshipper of our faithful God. Remember, we are not meant to bear our burdens alone.

- Be prepared for tears, but that's okay. You don't have to say anything particularly wise or wonderful. I've found that when people are in grief, they're not looking for someone to take all the pain away. They're just looking for someone to walk with them in the pain.

Statements to Avoid Saying

- "I know how you feel." Even if you've had a similar grief experience, none of us knows exactly how another person is feeling. We all process things differently.

- "Time heals all wounds." While it's true that the initial feelings of grief dissipate over time, when you hear "time heals all wounds," it can feel to your grieving friend that her pain is being minimized and taken lightly.

- "It's time for you get on with your life and start living again." This sometimes happens when the loved one had a lengthy illness. When your friend hears this statement, she may feel that you're asking her to forget her loved one. During this time, she needs to talk about her loved one, her memories, the funny things he said, etc. It's healthy and natural. In time, your friend will move on. But don't rush her.

- Comparing losses. If your friend has lost a child, avoid telling her about another person's loss and how their loss is more than hers. This is done in an effort to help the friend feel better—but it doesn't.

I hope these resources will help the next time you have a friend who is grieving.

NOTES

1. Martyn Lloyd-Jones, *Spiritual Depression: Its Causes and Cures* (Grand Rapids, Michigan: Eerdmans, 1965), 20.

2. John Piper, *When I Don't Desire God: How to Fight for Joy* (Crossway Books, 2004), 81.

3. John Piper, *Battling Unbelief* (Multnomah Publishers, 2007), 129-30.

4. Andrew Murray, *Abide in Christ* (First Rate Publishers, 1885).

5. Lillian Kwon, "Andy Stanley Responds to 'Why, God?' After Sandy Hook Shooting," www.christianpost.com/news, December 19, 2012.

6. Phillip Yancey, *Disappointment With God*, (Zondervan, 1997).

7. William Cowper, "God Moves in a Mysterious Way," (Public Domain, 1774).

8. Robert W. Kelleman, *God's Healing for Life's Losses*, (Winona Lake, IN, BMH Books, 2010).

9. Elvina Hall, John T. Grape, "Jesus Paid It All," (Public Domain, 1865).

10. Helen Lemmel, "Turn Your Eyes Upon Jesus," (Public Domain, 1922).

11. C.S. Lewis, *Letters to Malcolm Chiefly on Prayer*, (New York, Harcourt Brace Jovanovich, 1963), 89-90.

12. Joni Eareckson Tada, Interview with Larry King on *Larry King Live*, April, 2009.

13. Tony Dungy with Nathan Whitaker, *Quiet Strength: The Principles, Practice & Priorities of a Winning Life*, (Tyndale House Publishers, 2007).

14. Tony Dungy, *The Baptist Press*, Art Stricklin, February 3, 2006.

15. Alex Murashko, www.christianpost.com, "Saddleback Church Hosts Historic Gathering on Mental Health and the Church," March 29, 2014.

16. Kay Warren, Facebook post, March 13, 2014.

17. Rodney Francis, "Walking With a Limp," *The Gospel Faith Messenger Ministry*, www.gospel.org.nz, December 4, 2012.

18. Jennifer Rothschild, *God is Just Not Fair*, (Zondervan, 2014), 61-62.

19. Elvina M. Hall, John T. Grape, "Jesus Paid It All," (Public Domain, 1865).

20. Julia H. Johnston, Daniel B. Towner, "Grace Greater Than Our Sin," (Public Domain, 1922).

21. John Newton, "Amazing Grace," (Public Domain, 1779).

ABOUT THE AUTHOR

Connie Carey is an author, musician and award-winning speaker whose passion is helping others move beyond the lies that hold them back. Weaving messages with music and humor, she encourages, equips and inspires her audiences to think about their challenges from a radically renewed perspective.

An increasingly sought-after speaker in the corporate and church realm, she is a member of the National Speakers Association. In 2013, Connie was 1st runner up in the Semifinals of the World Championship of Public Speaking sponsored by Toastmasters International. Of 30,000 contestants from 122 countries, she emerged as one of the Top 18. Yet, somehow she can never find her keys. If you're looking for a speaker on organizing your life, hey, she's not the one.

Whether singing, sharing life-changing principles or just telling one of her side-splitting tales, audiences relate to her experiences, struggles and lessons.

Connie makes her home in Georgia with her husband, John and a cat they creatively named "Kitty". Marrying John transformed her overnight from single girl to grandmother...and she loves it.

Connie welcomes the opportunity to speak at your next event, seminar or conference. This particular message, Falling Up (complete with video of her skydiving experience!), can be delivered as a keynote or multi-message package. You can contact her at www.conniecarey.com.

Keep up with Connie Online: Get to know Connie and dialog with her through her blog, *Life. Lessons. Laughter.*, located at www.conniecarey.com, and on Facebook at Connie Mercer Carey.

Connie's Worship CD: Connie's CD, *Simply Instrumental*, is a perfect companion to your times of worship and reflection. Set a reflective mood with this collection of classic and new instrumental worship songs performed by pianist/flutist Connie Carey and woven with soothing violin. Songs include: "To God Be the Glory," "Friend of God/What a Friend We Have in Jesus," "How Great is Our God/How Great Thou Art," "Jesus Loves Me," "Amazing Grace" and more. CD can be purchased at www.conniecarey.com/shop.